GEORGE CHAPMAN

selected poems

edited by
Eirian Wain

Fyfield Books
Carcanet · Manchester

Note: the text of George Chapman's *Selected Poems* has been modernized by the publisher in accordance with the general style of Fyfield Books presentation.

Copyright © Eirian Wain 1978

SBN 85635 242 X

All Rights Reserved

First published 1978 by
Carcanet New Press Limited
330 Corn Exchange
Manchester M4 3BG

Printed in Great Britain by
Unwin Brothers Limited, Old Woking

CONTENTS

Introduction	7
Further Reading	19
Ovid's Banquet of Sense	21
A Coronet for his Mistress	34
De Guiana, Carmen Epicum	38
Hero and Leander	
The Third Sestiad	44
from *The Fifth Sestiad*	56
Peristeros: or the Male Turtle	57
from Euthymiae Raptus	58
The Iliads of Homer	
from *To the Reader*	74
from *The Sixth Book*	78
from Eugenia, or, True Nobility's Trance	83
Epilogue to the Hymns of Homer	87

INTRODUCTION

> Was it the proud full sail of his great verse,
> Bound for the prize of all too precious you,
> That did my ripe thoughts in my brain inhearse,
> Making their tomb the womb wherein they grew?
> Was it his spirit, by spirits taught to write
> Above a mortal pitch, that struck me dead?
> No, neither he, nor his compeers by night
> Giving him aid, my verse astonished.
> He, nor that affable familiar ghost
> Which nightly gulls him with intelligence,
> As victors of my silence cannot boast;
> I was not sick of any fear from thence:
> > But when your countenance fill'd up his line,
> > Then lack'd I matter; that enfeebled mine.

WHETHER George Chapman was indeed the rival poet of Shakespeare's Sonnets is still a matter of conjecture, but the most potent connection between them remains the similarity and impenetrability of their early lives. Chapman was born in Hitchin, Hertfordshire, in about 1559, the younger son of a farmer, but thereafter little is known of him until the publication of his first poem, *The Shadow of Night*, in 1593 at the comparatively late age of thirty-four. Anthony à Wood's assertion that 'he spent some time in Oxon, where he was observed to be most excellent in the Lat. and Greek tongues but not in logic and philosophy' seems to be gainsaid by Chapman's references through his work to himself as a self-taught man, and to scholars and academics who

> ever rate
> A man for learning,—with that estimate
> They made of him, when in the schools he liv'd;
> And how so ere he scatter'd since, or thriv'd,
> Still they esteem him as they held him then.

Wood continues: 'he settled in the metropolis where he became much admired of Edm. Spenser, S. Daniel, Wm. Shakespeare & Marlowe etc'.

7

Throughout his life Chapman was dogged by actions against him for the repayment of debts. One such action, undertaken in 1599, has helped to cast some light on his early life. In 1583, 'when in attendance on Sir Raphe Sadler Knyght then Chancellor of the Duchy of Lancaster, and Privy Councillor of Queen Elizabeth', he seems to have borrowed money from a certain John Wolfall. Sir Ralph Sadler, to whom Elizabeth often entrusted the custody of Mary Queen of Scots, owned, in addition to his other estates, a manor in the Hundred of Hitchin, Chapman's birthplace. John Wolfall's son, in answer to a Chancery bill brought against him by Chapman in 1608, stated that his father had not insisted on repayment of the debt until 1599 because: 'as well as the absence of the said Complainante beyond the seas, as the charitable disposition of his defendants father towards the said Complainante'. Perhaps Chapman's early manhood was spent, not in the university, but as page in the service of a local great landlord. It is tempting to conjecture that he left the employ of Sir Ralph Sadler to volunteer for service in the Low Countries, as did Ben Jonson and Sir Philip Sidney. Indeed there are many similarities between the latter's *Defence of Poesie* and Chapman's prose epistle prefaced to the first poem in this selection. Sidney's 'believe, with me, that there are many mysteries contained in Poetry which of purpose were written darkly, lest by profane wits it should be abused' is echoed by Chapman's

> Obscurity in affection of words and indigested conceits, is pedantical and childish; but where it shroudeth itself in the heart of his subject, uttered with fitness of figure and expressive epithets, with that darkness will I still labour to be shadowed. Rich minerals are digged out of the bowels of the earth, not found in the superficies and dust of it . . .

Much has been made of Chapman's obscurity even by those who love him. In his affectionate introduction to the poems, even Swinburne does not hesitate to lay that tawse about his shoulders; but I hope in this small selection to show that it is possible to read him not with pedantry but with pleasure. 'I know that empty, and dark spirits, will complain of palpable night: but those that beforehand, have a radiant, and light-bearing intellect, will say they can pass through Corinna's garden without the help of a lantern'.

One small lantern I wish to light. Chapman's so-called minor poems run to four hundred pages, his translation of Homer to a thousand; he was also a prolific dramatist. In Swinburne's phrase I might have 'gathered . . . large handfuls of fine verses, which when thus culled out and bound up into separate sheaves make a better show than in the text where they lay entangled among weeds and briars'. I have chosen rather to regard the 'weeds and briars' as the compost of fine flowers. Chapman's dramatic work has had to be omitted—*lucidius olim*. For the rest, I have tried to print extended passages, and to retain the argument and the shape of the original poems. Lovers of Chapman will appreciate my difficulties and, I hope, commend my labours.

In the prose letter dedicating *The Shadow of Night* to Matthew Roydon Chapman writes:

> I remember, my good Matthew, how joyfully oftentimes you reported unto me, that most ingenious Darby, deep-searching Northumberland, and skill-embracing heir of Hunsdon had most profitably entertained learning in themselves, to the vital warmth of freezing science, and to the admirable lustre of their true nobility, whose high-deserving virtues may cause me hereafter strike that fire out of darkness, which the brightest day shall envy for beauty . . .

Roydon, with Raleigh, Marlowe and the mathematician Thomas Harriot (to whom Chapman also dedicated a poem) made up a circle for scientific discussion which was castigated by a contemporary pamphleteer as 'Sir Walter Raleigh's School of Atheism'. In recent years many theories and much research have gone into proving that *Love's Labour's Lost* is a satirical attack on this circle, and upon Chapman himself. The same theory which presupposes Chapman to be Shakespeare's rival poet, finds many verbal echoes in the play as well as in the sonnet to confirm this supposition: 'Beauty is bought by judgment of the eye,/Not utter'd by base sale of chapmen's tongues.' In 'the hue of dungeons and the school of night' is there a conflation of 'the school of atheism' and *The Shadow of Night*? In the same epistle Chapman uses the phrase 'heavenly familiar'. Is the 'affable familiar ghost' Homer? Who are his 'compeers by night'?

The question-marks remain. All that is certain is that the play must have been written to ridicule just such a circle as Raleigh gathered about him, and that Chapman was certainly an aspiring if not an actual member of the *cénacle*. London in the last decade of the century witnessed an astonishing upsurge of poetry among that generation of brawling, adventurous, fantastical men. They must often have met in the tavern, in the theatre, in the great houses of the aristocrats to whom they dedicated their poems, in the court of the Queen for whom so often their plays were written and performed. In 1593 when the theatres were closed by an outbreak of plague, Shakespeare diverted his teeming imagination to the erotic epyllion and produced *Venus and Adonis*; Marlowe died in a tavern brawl leaving behind him the unfinished but already substantial *Hero and Leander*, which Chapman was to complete, very much in his own vein, but with no lowering of its high level of moral intensity.

In the meanwhile he was at work on his own epyllion, *Ovid's Banquet of Sense*. The title of course refers to Plato's *Symposium*, and particularly to Ficino's commentary upon it, published in 1482, and now believed to have been amongst Chapman's favourite reading. The neo-platonic doctrine of love is devoted to refinement of the five senses from the most earthy, touch, in an ascending order to hearing, and thence to reason; in the 'Argument' to Chapman's poem this order is re-arranged. John Buxton in his book *Elizabethan Taste* draws attention to Donatus's commentary on Terence's *Eunuchus*, in which the Five Lines of Love are defined as: *prima visus; secunda loqui; tertia tactus; quarta osculari; quinta coitus*; and suggests that Chapman used it as a counterpoint to the neo-platonic theme. Chapman does not wholly succeed in bringing this to a harmonious close: the Feast of Love is mentioned but not described, the tone is often marred by passages of the didactic reasoning which Chapman always found it hard to avoid, and the poem somewhat abruptly ends with Ovid's decision to write *The Art of Love*. Nevertheless it is full of Chapman's fine conceits, and the musical and sensuous writing which he was to bring to its highest pitch in his completion of *Hero and Leander*. In the same volume, perhaps as a coda to his erotic poem, he publishes a sequence of sonnets, *A Coronet for his Mistress Philosophy*, in which he addresses the 'Muses that sing love's sensual emperies', and ends with an attack upon his fellow writers 'that live by soothing moods, and serving times'. It is a theme which is to recur with increasing savagery throughout his work: his sense of isolation, of preserving in his own person the pure milk of an existence devoted to learning and the inward life, seems little mitigated by his success as a dramatist, by the friendship of Ben Jonson, by the patronage of noblemen and princes.

He remained loyal to Sir Walter Raleigh even when the latter was out of favour with the Queen, and had been replaced by the Earl of Essex. In Raleigh's circle was Laurence Keymis, the explorer and mathematician; together they were to make three voyages of exploration to Guiana. After the second journey Keymis wrote *A Relation of the Second Voyage to Guiana*, and published it in 1596 prefixed by a poem by Chapman, *De Guiana, Carmen Epicum*. The Queen refused to see Raleigh on his return from the first voyage and would not finance any subsequent explorations. Chapman's poem is a passionate, courageous and probably foolhardy attempt to persuade Elizabeth to change her mind. Although it is subtitled *Carmen Epicum* there is no narrative in the poem. It is his only poem in blank verse, although each swell of the argument ends with a rhyming couplet. His eloquence seems not to have moved the Queen; Keymis and Raleigh were later imprisoned in the Tower, and it was not until the reign of James that they made their final voyage to Guiana. Unfortunately Raleigh's son was killed, and Keymis, distressed by Sir Walter's displeasure and grief, took his own life. Raleigh's own account of the voyage was published in Hakluyt, and the journal of the final journey has been published in recent years. Chapman's poem is now interesting, less for its literary merits than for the light it throws on the main body of his work.

We cannot know when Chapman began his continuation of *Hero and Leander*. The tone, the lyrical intensity, the suppleness of the narrative, the fine conceits are all at one with his *Banquet of Sense*. He may have read the poem in manuscript before the death of his friend whom he addresses in a highly charged passage within the poem as

> thou most strangely-intellectual fire,
> That proper to my soul hast power t'inspire

> Her burning faculties, and with the wings
> Of thy unspheared flame visit'st the springs
> Of spirits immortal; now (as swift as time
> Doth follow motion) find th'eternal clime
> Of his free soul, whose living subject stood
> Up to the chin in the Pierian flood,
> And drunk to me half this Musean storie,
> Inscribing it to deathless memorie:
> Confer with it, and make my pledge as deep,
> That neithers draught be consecrate to sleep.
> Tell it how much his late desires I tender,
> (If yet it know not) and to light surrender
> My soul's dark offspring, willing it should die
> To loves, to passions, and society.

The story, taken from Musaeus, is of two lovers living on either shore of the Hellespont, Hero the priestess of Aphrodite in Sestos, Leander in Abydos. Guided by Hero's torch, Leander swims the Hellespont at night and persuades her to

> Abandon fruitless cold virginity,
> The gentle Queen of love's sole enemy.
> Then shall you most resemble Venus' nun
> When Venus' sweet rites are perform'd and done.

Chapman takes up the story in the third sestiad, when Leander—their love consummated—swims back across the Hellespont with 'sweet Hero left upon her bed alone'. To him appears the goddess Ceremony, a fine imaginative creation of the poet's, which it is essential to comprehend if we are to grasp the general tenor of Chapman's part of the poem. She is Thesme 'deity sovereign of customs and religious rites', the companion of Devotion, Order, State and Reverence, and the enemy of Avarice and Barbarism. Crowned with all the stars, wearing about her neck 'a rich disparent pentacle', preceded by divine music,

> she sharply did reprove
> Leander's bluntness in his violent love;
> Told him how poor was substance without rites
> Like bills unsign'd; desires without delights.

C. S. Lewis writes, 'I do not know any passage more quintessentially

Elizabethan. It is linked up with so much in Shakespeare and Spenser, in the *Arcadia*, in Hall's chronicle; in their emblems and gardening and the conduct of their public life: in their very cosmology and theology'.

There follows a lyrical and imaginative analysis of Hero's state of mind: 'Love is a golden bubble, full of dreams,/That waking breaks, and fills us with extremes.' Her mood veers from remorse to despair to passionate longing for the body of her lover. Chapman combines the insight and compassion of a great novelist with the rich imagery, the fantastical allegory, even the didacticism typical of the age. Finally she resolves to dissimulate, and the poet observes but does not condemn the desperate sophistry of the arguments which she uses to justify her actions to herself.

The fourth sestiad of the poem, not given here, is devoted to the sacrificial rites which Hero performs in an attempt to mollify the goddess Venus. Venus appears, rejects her sacrifice, and invokes Eronusis, the goddess of Dissimulation, another creation of Chapman's worthy to be part of *The Faerie Queen*. Hero, still longing for Leander, and seeking to enjoy by proxy the love which will not be hers until the fall of night, sends for two betrothed lovers whom she before had refused to marry. In the feast that follows their marriage, 'the wild nymph Teras' sings the beautiful 'Epithalamion' which is the most lovely piece of lyric writing in all Chapman's work. Hero and Leander are not to meet again in human form. In the final sestiad, though Leucote, Venus's swan, has prayed for clemency, the Fates stir up the winds, 'the guilty Hellespont is mix'd and stain'd with bloody torrents' as Leander swims across it, Hero's torch is blown out and she throws herself into the sea to perish with her lover. Here Chapman achieves his final act of compassion: he turns the lovers into birds—'thistlewarps' who fly far away from any sea, feeding on thistle tops to remind them of sorrows past. 'They were the first that ever poet sung'.

In this same year Chapman published his first stage play, a comedy with the somewhat unlikely title *The Blind Beggar of Alexandria*; and the first instalment of his best-known work, the translation of Homer. Nevertheless he is as always, it seems, short of money. The translation of the first five books of the *Iliad* is dedicated with his usual uncannily bad sense of timing, to the Earl of Essex. In it he complains of his straitened circumstances, and in 1599 he was for a short time actually imprisoned for his debt to John Wolfall. That year another comedy, then silence. He reappears as a contributor to 'the poetical essays' written to accompany the long allegorical poem *Love's Martyr* written by Robert Chester. The theme of the poem is the mating of the Phoenix and the Turtle, largely remembered for Shakespeare's contribution now known by that name. Chapman's poem, to which he gives the title *Peristeros, or the Male Turtle*, is not one of his best poems. Shorter forms seem not to have suited the extended and elaborated conceit which came most naturally to him. Compression often resulted in clumsiness and distortion.

Two years later the old Queen is dead, James is on the throne, and Chapman entered what was probably the happiest period of his life. The young heir to the throne, Prince Henry, surrounded himself with a gathering of talents: musicians; the architect Inigo Jones; and many writers, among them Chapman, now becoming well-known as a dramatist, the friend and collaborator of Ben Jonson. The young prince encouraged him in his work, particularly in his translation of Homer, and appointed him to a minor position in

> his spring-court; where all the prime spirits met
> Of all our kingdoms; as if from death
> That in men living, baseness and rapine sheath,
> Where they before lived, they unwares were come
> Into a free and fresh Elysium . . .

Even so his ill fortune did not wholly desert him. King James caused him and his collaborators Jonson and Marston to be imprisoned for a supposedly slighting reference to the Scots in their play *Eastward Ho*. They were soon released on the intervention of the lords Salisbury and Suffolk, and this may account for Chapman's blind loyalty later in life to the wife of the Earl of Somerset, Suffolk's daughter. Chapman's old friends and patrons, Raleigh and Northumberland, were imprisoned in the Tower for supposed implication in the Gunpowder Plot: among the three English books which the earl took with him was his copy of Chapman's translation of Homer. Three years later 'only the principal person, the author, escaped' when the French ambassador, protesting against the portrayal of the French

King in Chapman's *Tragedy of Biron*, caused some of the actors to be imprisoned.

None of this seems to have lost him the affectionate support of Prince Henry, and in 1609 Chapman dedicated to him the long poem *Euthymiae Raptus; or the Teares of Peace*. It is a long and difficult poem, both in form and argument, but it is central to an understanding of Chapman's mind. Euthymia is his own coinage from the Greek, and appears to mean the contentment of mind that comes from inward peace, combined with the peace of a respite between warring nations.

Homer was 'angel to me, star and fate'. In this poem he is Chapman's mentor, as Virgil was to Dante, and reveals to him his vision of Peace. The action takes place 'in his native air; and on the hill next Hitchin's left hand'. Peace is 'a lady, like a Deity indew'd, but weeping like a woman'. Beneath her arm she carries the coffin of dead Love, accompanied by her children, the Muses, the Virtues, the Graces, and lastly Religion. In answer to Chapman, who is the interlocutor, Peace reveals her 'tears', which consist both of her lamentations on the death of Love, and her thoughts on the causes of war: man's refusal to set aside outward shows, and to direct his mind to learning and to God. Into this strand of Chapman's stoical philosophy are woven his neo-platonism and an element of strange Spenserian allegory. The golden light which suffused *Hero and Leander* and *The Banquet of Sense* has here become a fitful darkness lit by stormy lightning, and the muttering of the thunder of his condemnation of the world in which he lives.

Two years later the Prince is dead.

> Blest yet, and sacred shalt thy memory be,
> O nothing-less-than-mortal Deity.
> Thy graces like the Sun, to all men giving;
> Fatal to thee in death, but kill me living.
> Now as inverted like th'Antipodes
> The world (in all things of desert to please)
> Is fall'n on us with thee; thy ruins lie
> On our burst bosoms, as if from the sky
> The Day-star, greater than the world were driven
> Sunk to the earth, and left a hole in heaven.

The *Epicede on Prince Henry*, written in 1612, from which these lines are taken, is dedicated to 'my affectionate and true friend, Mr Henry Jones'. From 1610 to 1612, Henry Jones had been helping Chapman with 'ready money out of his purse', for the poet 'was a pleasant witty fellow and one whom this deponent delighted and loved'. In the year of the Prince's death, Jones was leaving to live in Ireland, and presented Chapman with a bill for £100. The unfortunate poet admitted the liability and a bond for the amount which was guaranteed by his brother Thomas Chapman, who had inherited their father's small estate and was now 'a man of good wealth'. The subsequent proceedings in the Court of Chancery are of exquisite complexity, and were to last for nearly ten years. Their only interest lies in the light which they cast upon the poet's later life. One lawyer enquires whether Chapman 'is not a poet, or one that doth profess poetry'. A deposition of 1617 states that Chapman 'is of mean and poor estate' and 'doth now live in remote places and is hard to be found'. An earlier creditor had written of him as someone 'who at the first being a man of very good parts and expectation hath sithence very unadvisedly spent the most part of his time and his estate in fruitless and vain poetry'. Chapman seems certainly to have retired from London, perhaps to his brother's estate in Hitchin. He makes occasional returns to the capital, but there is general agreement that he ceased to work as a dramatist from that time.

His relations with his royal and noble patrons appear equally unfortunate. Though he was commissioned to write a Masque of the Middle Temple for the marriage of King James's daughter Elizabeth to the Elector Palatinate in 1613, in the same year he is writing to the Master of the Rolls asking for payment for a masque of which he was the 'sole writer, and in part, inventor' and for which he had 'suffered loss of reputation, want and imprisonment'. He viewed with genuine amazement the storm occasioned by his poem *Andromeda Liberata* (incidentally one of his worst) written on the occasion of the marriage of Robert Carr, Earl of Somerset, to the one-time wife of the Earl of Essex, whose marriage had been annulled. In the legend, Andromeda is released by Perseus from the rock to which she had been chained; Chapman's contemporaries assumed that he intended the rock to be Essex. Chapman published a pained justification in prose which contains an interesting analysis of his own interpretation of allegory. With the same courage with which he had defended Raleigh, he remained loyal to the couple even when they were imprisoned in the Tower for their alleged murder of Sir Thomas Overbury, and dedicated to Somerset his translation of the *Odyssey* and the *Hymns* of Homer with an 'Epistle Dedicatory' to 'my ever most-worthy-to-be-most-honoured Lord'.

Perhaps recalling his own service in the Netherlands he wrote an epicede on the death of 'the most religiously noble William Lord Russell', a one-time commander in the Netherlands, who had succeeded Sir Philip Sidney as Governor of Flushing. The splendid bestiary forms part of the 'Inductio' to *Eugenia: or True Nobility's Trance*. This is followed by three vigils: in a dedicatory letter to Francis Russell, Chapman promises to compose a vigil on every anniversary of his father's death, but as far as is known these were never undertaken.

In 1616 the *Iliad* and the *Odyssey* are complete, and published as *The Whole Works of Homer*, with an impressive engraving of Chapman's head as frontispiece: 'The work that I was born to do, is done'. In the address 'To the Reader', prefixed to his translation of the *Iliad*, Chapman justifies his use of fourteeners, 'for this long poem asks this length of verse', but he was of course later to change his mind, and the *Odyssey* is translated into heroic couplets. 'To the Reader' is worth reading for Chapman's views on translation. I have no space here for a discussion of the merits of his translation. Many critics have closely analysed his dependence on the Spondanus text issued in 1583 with a Latin translation in parallel columns prepared by Andreas Divus. The arguments heading the various books are taken directly from Spondanus. Undoubtedly Chapman shows a great deal of skill in varying the caesura within the lines, and in avoiding the over-regular division into sixes and eights which is one of the pitfalls of this metre.

Ben Jonson's copy of Chapman's translation, now in the Fitzwilliam Museum, is annotated in the margins with criticism of his old friend's scholarship. In his verses prefixed to Jonson's *Sejanus*, Chapman had written:

> And so, good friend, safe passage to thy freight,
> To thee a long peace, through a virtuous strife,

> In which let's both contend to virtue's height,
> Not making Fame our object, but good life.

Sadly, towards the end of their friendship this had been replaced by 'An Invective written by Mr George Chapman against Mr Ben Jonson', unfinished, never published during his lifetime and found in a commonplace-book preserved among the Ashmole manuscripts in the Bodleian.

> Great, learned witty Ben, be pleased to light
> The world with that three-forked fire; nor fright
> All us, thy sublearn'd, with luciferous boast
> That thou art most great, most learn'd, witty most
> Of all the kingdom, nay of all the earth;
> As being a thing betwixt a human birth
> And an infernal.

And so on for two hundred lines, none of which were probably meant for the eyes of his witty Ben.

George Chapman died in 1634. He is buried in the Church of St Giles in the Fields in London. Let this, written for his friend John Fletcher, be his epitaph:

> This iron age that eats itself, will never
> Bite at your golden world; that others, ever
> Loved as itself: then like your books do you
> Live in old peace: and that for praise allow.

FURTHER READING

The Complete Poems of George Chapman, ed. Phyllis Bartlett, New York, 1941.

Chapman's Homer: the Iliad, the Odyssey and the lesser Homerica, ed. Allardyce Nicoll, London, 1957.

Franck L. Schoell, *Etudes sur l'Humanisme Continental en Angleterre à la Fin de la Renaissance*, Paris, 1926.

J. Robertson, 'The Early Life of George Chapman', *Modern Language Review*, vol. 40, 1945.

Mark Eccles, 'Chapman's Early Years', *Studies in Philology*, vol. 43, 1946.

C. J. Sisson and Robert Butman, 'George Chapman, 1612-22. Some New Facts', *Modern Language Review*, vol. 46, 1951.

D. J. Gordon, 'Chapman's *Hero and Leander*', *English Miscellany*, Rome, 1954.

OVID'S BANQUET OF SENSE

To the truly learned, and my worthy friend,
Master Matthew Roydon.

Such is the wilful poverty of judgements (sweet Master) wandering like passportless men, in contempt of the divine discipline of Poesy, that a man may well fear to frequent their walks. The profane multitude I hate, and only consecrate my strange poems to these searching spirits, whom learning hath made noble, and nobility sacred; endeavouring that material oration, which you call *schema*; varying in some rare fiction, from popular custom, even for the pure sakes of ornament and utility; this of Euripides exceeding sweetly relishing with me: *lentem coquens ne quicquam olentis addito*.

But that Poesy should be as pervial as oratory, and plainness her special ornament, were the plain way to barbarism: and to make the ass run proud of his ears; to take away strength from lions, and give camels horns.

That *Enargia* or clearness of representation, required in absolute poems is not the perspicuous delivery of a low invention; but high, and hearty invention expressed in most significant, and unaffected phrase; it serves not a skilful painter's turn, to draw the figure of a face only to make known who it represents; but he must limn it, give lustre, shadow, and heightening; which though ignorants will esteem spiced, and too curious, yet such as have the judicial perspective, will see it hath motion, spirit and life.

There is no confection made to last, but it is admitted more cost and skill than presently to be used simples; and in my opinion, that which being with a little endeavour searched, adds a kind of majesty to Poesy; is better than that which every cobbler may sing to his patch.

Obscurity in affection of words, and indigested conceits, is pedantical and childish; but where it shroudeth itself in the heart of his subject, uttered with fitness of figure, and expressive epithets; with that darkness will I still labour to be shadowed: rich minerals are digged out of the bowels of the earth, not found in the superficies and dust of it; charms made of unlearned characters are not consecrate by the muses which are divine artists, but by Euippes' daughters, that challenged them with mere nature, whose breasts I doubt not had been well worthy commendation, if their comparison had not turned them into [mag] pies.

Thus (not affecting glory for mine own slight labours, but desirous others should be more worthily glorious, nor professing sacred Poesy in any degree,) I thought good to submit to your apt judgement: acquainted long since with the true habit of Poesy, and now since your labouring wits endeavour heaven-high thoughts of nature, you have actual means to sound the philosophical conceits, that my new pen so seriously courteth. I know that empty, and dark spirits, will complain of palpable night: but those that beforehand, have a radiant, and light-bearing intellect, will say they can pass through Corinna's garden without the help of a lantern.

Your own most worthily and sincerely affected
GEORGE CHAPMAN

The Argument

Ovid, newly enamoured of Julia, (daughter to Octavius Augustus Caesar, after by him called Corinna,) secretly conveyed himself into a garden of the emperor's court: in an arbour whereof, Corinna was bathing; playing upon her lute, and singing: which Ovid overhearing, was exceedingly pleased with the sweetness of her voice, and to himself uttered the comfort he conceived in his sense of hearing. AUDITUS

Then the odours she used in her bath, breathing a rich savour, he expresseth the joy he felt in his sense of smelling. OLFACTUS

Thus growing more deeply enamoured, in great contentation with himself, he ventures to see her in the pride of her nakedness: which doing by stealth, he discovered the comfort he conceived in seeing, and the glory of her beauty. VISUS

Not yet satisfied, he useth all his art to make known

his being there, without her offence: or (being necessarily offended) to appease her: which done, he entreats a kiss to serve for satisfaction of his taste, which he obtains.   GUSTUS

Then proceeds he to entreaty for the fifth sense and there is interrupted.   TACTUS

Narratio

7   In a loose robe of tinsel forth she came,
     Nothing but it betwixt her nakedness
     And envious light. The downward-burning flame
     Of her rich hair did threaten new access,
         Of vent'rous Phaeton to scorch the fields:
     And thus to bathing came our Poet's goddess,
         Her handmaids bearing all things pleasure yields
     To such a service; odours most delighted,
     And purest linen which her looks had whited.

8   Then cast she off her robe, and stood upright,
     As lightning breaks out of a labouring cloud;
     Or as the morning heaven casts off the night,
     Or as that heaven cast off itself, and show'd
         Heaven's upper light, to which the brightest day
     Is but a black and melancholy shroud:
         Or as when Venus striv'd for sovereign sway
     Of charmful beauty, in young Troy's desire,
     So stood Corinna vanishing her tire.

11   And now she used the fount, where Niobe,
     Tomb'd in herself, poured her lost soul in tears,
     Upon the bosom of this Roman Phoebe;
     Who, bath'd and odour'd; her bright limbs she rears,
         And drying her on that disparent ground;
     Her lute she takes t'enamour heavenly ears,
         And try if with her voice's vital sound,
     She could warm life through those cold statues spread,
     And cheer the dame that wept when she was dead.

12   And thus she sung, all naked as she sat,
      Laying the happy lute upon her thigh,
      Not thinking any near to wonder at
      The bliss of her sweet breasts' divinity.

>   The song of CORINNA
>*'Tis better to contemn than love,*
>*And to be fair than wise;*
>*For souls are ruled by eyes:*
>*And Jove's bird, seiz'd by Cypris' dove,*
>*It is our grace and sport to see,*
>*Our beauty's sorcery,*
>*That makes (like destiny)*
>*Men follow us the more we flee;*
>*That sets wise glosses on the fool,*
>*And turns her cheeks to books,*
>*Where wisdom sees in looks*
>*Derision laughing at his school,*
>   *Who (loving) proves, prophaneness, holy;*
>   *Nature, our fate, our wisdom, folly.*

13   While this was singing, Ovid young in love
      With her perfections, never proving yet
      How merciful a mistress she would prove,
      Boldly embrac'd the power he could not let
         And like a fiery exhalation
      Followed the sun, he wish'd might never set;
         Trusting herein his constellation
      Rul'd by love's beams, which Julia's eyes erected,
      Whose beauty was the star his life directed.

15   Whereat his wit, assumed fiery wings,
      Soaring above the temper of his soul,
      And he the purifying rapture sings
      Of his ears' sense, takes full the Thespian bowl
         And it carouseth to his mistress' health,
      Whose sprightful verdure did dull flesh control,

       And his conceit he crowneth with the wealth
       Of all the Muses in his pleased senses,
       When with the ears' delight he thus commences:

16 Now Muses come, repair your broken wings,
     (Pluck'd, and prophan'd by rustic ignorance,)
    With feathers of these notes my Mistress sings;
    And let quick verse her drooping head advance
        From dungeons of contempt to smite the stars;
    In Julia's tunes, led forth by furious trance,
        A thousand muses come to bid you wars,
    Dive to your spring, and hide you from the stroke,
    All poets' furies will her tunes invoke.

17 Never was any sense so set on fire
    With an immortal ardour, as mine ears;
    Her fingers to the strings doth speech inspire
    And number'd laughter; that the descant bears
        To her sweet voice; whose species through my sense
    My spirits to their highest function rears;
        To which impress'd with ceaseless confluence
    It useth them, as proper to her power
    Marries my soul, and makes itself her dower;

18 Methinks her tunes fly gilt, like Attic bees
    To my ears' hives, with honey tried to air;
    My brain is but the comb, the wax, the lees,
    My soul the drone, that lives by their affair.
        O so it sweets, refines, and ravisheth,
    And with what sport they sting in their repair:
        Rise then in swarms, and sting me thus to death
    Or turn me into swound; possess me whole,
    Soul to my life, and essence to my soul.

19 Say gentle Air, O does it not thee good
    Thus to be smit with her correcting voice?
    Why dance ye not, ye daughters of the wood?
    Wither for ever, if not now rejoice,

   Rise stones, and build a city with her notes,
And notes infuse with your most Cynthian noise,
  To all the trees, sweet flowers, and crystal floats,
That crown, and make this cheerful garden quick,
Virtue, that every touch may make them music.

20 O that as man is call'd a little world
The world might shrink into a little man,
To hear the notes about this garden hurl'd,
That skill disperst in tunes so Orphean
  Might not be lost in smiting stocks and trees
That have no ears; but grown as it began
  Spread their renowns, as far as Phoebus sees
Through earth's dull veins; that she like heaven might move,
In ceaseless music, and be fill'd with love.

31 Herewith, as Ovid something nearer drew,   OLFACTUS
Her odours, odour'd with her breath and breast,
Into the censer of his savour flew,
As if the phoenix hasting to her rest
  Had gather'd all th'Arabian spicery
T'embalm her body in her tomb, her nest,
  And there lay burning 'gainst Apollo's eye,
Whose fiery air straight piercing Ovid's brain
Inflam'd his Muse with a more odorous vein.

32 And thus he sung, Come sovereign odours, come
Restore my spirits now in love consuming,
Wax hotter air, make them more savoursome,
My fainting life with fresh-breath'd soul perfuming,
  The flames of my disease are violent,
And many perish on late helps presuming,
  With which hard fate must I yet stand content,
As odours put in fire most richly smell,
So men must burn in love that will excell.

33 And as the air is rarified with heat
But thick and gross with summer-killing cold,

So men in love aspire perfection's seat,
When others, slaves to base desire are sold,
   And if that men near Ganges liv'd by scent
Of flow'rs, and trees, more I a thousand fold
   May live by these pure fumes that do present
My Mistress' quick'ning, and consuming breath
Where her wish flies with power of life and death.

34 Methinks, as in these liberal fumes I burn
     My Mistress' lips be near with kiss-entices,
     And that which way soever I can turn,
     She turns withal, and breathes on me her spices,
        As if too pure for search of human eye
     She flew in air disburthening Indian prizes,
        And made each earthly fume to sacrifice.
     With her choice breath fell Cupid blows his fire,
     And after, burns himself in her desire.

35 Gentle, and noble are their tempers fram'd,
     That can be quicken'd with perfumes and sounds,
     And they are cripple-minded, gout-wit lam'd,
     That lie like fire-fit blocks, dead without wounds,
        Stirr'd up with nought, but hell-descending gain,
     The soul of fools that all their souls confounds,
        The art of peasants and our nobles' stain,
     The bane of virtue and the bliss of sin.
     Which none but fools and peasants glory in.

36 Sweet sounds and odours, are the heavens, on earth
     Where virtues live, of virtuous men deceas'd,
     Which in such like, receive their second birth
     By smell and hearing endlessly increas'd;
        They were mere flesh were not with them delighted,
     And every such is perish'd like a beast
        As all they shall that are so foggy-sprited,
     Odours feed love, and love clear heaven discovers,
     Lovers wear sweets then; sweetest minds, be lovers.

49 This said, he charg'd the arbour with his eye,   VISUS
   Which pierc'd it through, and at her breasts reflected,
   Striking him to the heart with ecstasy:
   As do the sun-beams 'gainst the earth prorected,
      With their reverberate vigour mount in flames,
   And burn much more than where they were directed,
      He saw th'extraction of all fairest dames:
   The fair of beauty, as whole countries come
   And show their riches in a little room.

51 This beauty's fair is an enchantment made
   By nature's witchcraft, tempting men to buy
   With endless shows, what endlessly will fade,
   Yet promise chapmen all eternity:
      But like to goods ill got a fate it hath,
   Brings men enrich'd therewith to beggary
      Unless th'enricher be as rich in faith,
   Enamour'd (like good self-love) with her own,
   Seen in another, then 'tis heaven alone.

56 With this digression, we will now return
   To Ovid's prospect in his fancy's storm:
   He thought he saw the arbour's bosom burn,
   Blaz'd with a fire wrought in a lady's form:
      Where silver pass'd the least: and nature's vaunt
   Did such a precious miracle perform,
      She lay, and seem'd a flood of diamant
   Bounded in flesh: as still as vesper's hair
   When not an aspen leaf is stirred with air.

57 She lay at length, like an immortal soul
   At endless rest in blest Elysium:
   And then did true felicity enrol
   So fair a lady, figure of her kingdom.
      Now Ovid's Muse as in her tropic shin'd,
   And he (struck dead) was mere heaven-born become,
      So his quick verse in equal height was shrin'd:

Or else blame me as his submitted debtor,
That never mistress had to make me better.

68 O Beauty, how attractive is thy pow'r?
For as the life's heat clings about the heart
So all men's hungry eyes do haunt thy bow'r,
Reigning in Greece, Troy swum to thee in art;
    Remov'd to Troy, Greece follow'd thee in fears;
Thou drew'st each sireless sword, each childless dart
    And pulld'st the tow'rs of Troy about thine ears:
Shall I then muse that thus thou drawest me?
No, but admire, I stand thus far from thee.

69 Herewith she rose like the autumnal star
Fresh burnish'd in the lofty ocean flood,
That darts his glorious influence more far
Than any lamp of bright Olympus' brood;
    She lifts her lightning arms above her head,
And stretcheth a meridian from her blood,
    That slept awake in her Elysian bed:
Then knit she up, lest loose, her glowing hair
Should scorch the centre and incense the air.

70 Thus when her fair heart-binding hands had tied
Those liberal tresses, her high frontier part,
She shrunk in curls, and curiously plied
Into the figure of a swelling heart:
    And then with jewels of device, it grac'd:
One was a sun graven at his even's depart,
    And under that a man's huge shadow plac'd,
Wherein was writ, in sable charactery,
Decrescente nobilitate, crescunt obscuri.

71 Another was an eye in sapphire set,
And close upon it a fresh laurel spray,
The skilful posy was, *Medio caret,*
To show not eyes, but means must truth display.

      The third was an Apollo with his team
About a dial and a world in way,
      The motto was, *Teipsum et orbem*,
Graven in the dial; these exceeding rare
And other like accomplements she ware.
. . .
Which for his fourth course made our poet court her.

87 This motion of my soul, my fantasy   GUSTUS
    Created by three senses put in act,
    Let justice nourish with my sympathy,
    Putting my other senses into fact,
        If now thou grant not, now chang'd that offence;
    To suffer change, doth perfect sense compact:
        Change then, and suffer for the use of sense,
    We live not for our selves, the ear, and eye,
    And every sense, must serve society.

88 To furnish then, this banquet where the taste
    Is never us'd, and yet the cheer divine,
    The nearest mean dear Mistress that thou hast
    To bless me with it, is a kiss of thine,
        Which grace shall borrow organs of my touch
    T'advance it to that inward taste of mine
        Which makes all sense, and shall delight as much
    Then with a kiss (dear life) adorn thy feast
    And let (as banquets should) the last be best.

97 Her moving towards him, made Ovid's eye
    Believe the firmament was coming down
    To take him quick to immortality,
    And that th'ambrosian kiss set on the crown:
        She spake in kissing, and her breath infus'd
    Restoring syrup in his taste, in swoon:
        And he imagin'd Hebe's hands had bruis'd
    A banquet of the Gods into his sense,
    Which fill'd him with this furious influence.

98   The motion of the heavens that did beget
        The golden age, and by whose harmony
        Heaven is preserv'd, in me on work is set,
        All instruments of deepest melody
            Set sweet in my desires to my love's liking
        With this sweet kiss in me their tunes apply,
            As if the best musicians' hands were striking:
        This kiss in me hath endless music clos'd,
        Like Phoebus' lute, on Nisus' towers impos'd.

99   And as a pebble cast into a spring,
        We see a sort of trembling circles rise,
        One forming other in their issuing
        Till over all the fount they circulize,
            So this perpetual-motion-making kiss,
        Is propagate through all my faculties,
            And makes my breast an endless fount of bliss,
        Of which, if Gods could drink, their matchless fare
        Would make them much more blessed than they are.

102   Then sacred Madam, since my other senses   TACTUS
        Have in your graces tasted such content,
        Let wealth not to be spent, fear no expenses,
        But give thy bounty true eternizement:
            Making my senses' ground-work, which is, feeling,
        Effect the other, endless excellent,
            Their substance with flint-softning softness stealing:
        Then let me feel, for know sweet beauty's Queen,
        Dames may be felt, as well as heard or seen.

105   Herewith, even glad his arguments to hear,
        Worthily willing to have lawful grounds
        To make the wond'rous power of heaven appear,
        In nothing more than her perfections found,
            Close to her navel she her mantle wrests,
        Slacking it upwards, and the folds unwound,
            Showing Latona's twins, her plenteous breasts

> The sun and Cynthia in their triumph-robes
> Of lady-skin; more rich than both their globes.

110 ... he laid his hand upon her side,
Which made her start like sparkles from a fire,
Or like Saturnia from th'ambrosian pride
Of her morn's slumber, frighted with admire
> When Jove laid young Alcides to her breast,
So startled she, not with a coy retire,
> But with the tender temper she was blest,
Proving her sharp, undull'd with handling yet,
Which keener edge on Ovid's longing set.

111 And feeling still, he sigh'd out this effect;
Alas why lent not heaven the soul a tongue?
Nor language, nor peculiar dialect,
To make her high conceits as highly sung,
> But that a fleshly engine must unfold
A spiritual notion; birth from princes sprung
> Peasants must nurse, free virtue wait on gold
And a profess'd though flattering enemy,
Must plead my honour, and my liberty.

112 O nature how dost thou defame in this
Our human honours? yoking men with beasts
And noblest minds with slaves? thus beauty's bliss,
Love and all virtues that quick spirit feasts
> Surfeit on flesh; and thou that banquet'st minds,
Most bounteous Mistress, of thy dull-tongu'd guests
> Reap'st not due thanks; thus rude frailty binds
What thou giv'st wings; thus joys I feel in thee
Hang on thy lips and will not uttered be.

113 Sweet touch the engine that love's bow doth bend,
The sense wherewith he feels him deified,
The object whereto all his actions tend,
In all his blindness his most pleasing guide,

> For thy sake will I write the Art of Love,
> Since thou dost blow his fire and feed his pride
> > Since in thy sphere his health and life doth move,
> For thee I hate who hate society
> And such as self-love makes his slavery.

114 In these dog-days how this contagion smothers
The purest bloods with virtue's diet fin'd
Nothing their own, unless they be some other's
Spite of themselves, are in themselves confin'd
> And live so poor they are of all despis'd,
> Their gifts, held down with scorn should be divin'd,
> > And they like mummers mask, unknown, unpris'd:
> A thousand marvels mourn in some such breast
> Would make a kind and worthy patron blest.

115 To me (dear Sovereign) thou art Patroness,
And I, with that thy graces have infus'd,
Will make all fat and foggy brains confess,
Riches may from a poor verse be deduc'd:
> And that gold's love shall leave them grovelling here,
> When thy perfections shall to heaven be mus'd,
> > Deck'd in bright verse, where angels shall appear
> The praise of virtue, love, and beauty singing,
> Honour to noblesse, shame to avarice bringing.

116 Here Ovid interrupted with the view
Of other dames, who then the garden painted,
Shrouded himself, and did as death eschew
All note by which his love's fame might be tainted:
> And as when mighty Macedon had won
> The monarchy of earth, yet when he fainted,
> > Grieved that no greater action could be done,
> And that there were no more worlds to subdue,
> So love's defects, love's conqueror did rue.

117 But as when expert painters have display'd,
To quickest life a monarch's royal hand

    Holding a sceptre, there is yet bewray'd
But half his fingers; when we understand
        The rest not to be seen; and never blame
The painter's art, in nicest censures scann'd:
        So in the compass of this curious frame,
Ovid well knew there was much more intended,
With whose omission none must be offended.

A CORONET FOR HIS MISTRESS
Philosophy

1   Muses that sing love's sensual empery,
        And lovers kindling your enraged fires
        At Cupid's bonfires burning in the eye,
        Blown with the empty breath of vain desires,
    You that prefer the painted cabinet
        Before the wealthy jewels it doth store ye,
        That all your joys in dying figures set,
        And stain the living substance of your glory,
    Abjure those joys, abhor their memory,
        And let my love the honour'd subject be
        Of love, and honour's complete history;
        Your eyes were never yet, let in to see
    The majesty and riches of the mind,
    But dwell in darkness; for your god is blind.

2   But dwell in darkness, for your god is blind,
        Humour pours down such torrents on his eyes,
        Which (as from mountains) fall on his base kind,
        And eat your entrails out with ecstasies.
    Colour, (whose hands for faintness are not felt)
        Can bind your waxen thoughts in adamant,
        And with her painted fires your hearts doth melt
        Which beat your souls in pieces with a pant,
    But my love is the cordial of souls
        Teaching by passion what perfection is,

      In whose fix'd beauties shine the sacred scrolls,
        And long-lost records of your human bliss
Spirit to flesh, and soul to spirit giving,
Love flows not from my liver, but her living.

3   Love flows not from my liver but her living,
        From whence all stings to perfect love are darted
        All pow'r, and thought of prideful lust depriving,
        Her life so pure and she so spotless hearted,
    In whom sits beauty with so firm a brow
        That age, nor care, nor torment can contract it;
        Heaven's glories shining there, do stuff allow,
        And virtue's constant graces do compact it.
    Her mind (the beam of God) draws in the fires
        Of her chaste eyes, from all earth's tempting fuel;
        Which upward lifts the looks of her desires
        And makes each precious thought in her a jewel,
    And as huge fires compress'd more proudly flame
    So her close beauties further blaze her fame.

4   So her close beauties further blaze her fame;
        When from the world, into herself reflected
        She lets her (shameless) glory in her shame
        Content for heav'n to be of earth rejected,
    She thus depress'd, knocks at Olympus' gate,
        And in th'untainted temple of her heart
        Doth the divorceless nuptials celebrate
        'Twixt god and her; where love's prophaned dart
    Feeds the chaste flames of Hymen's firmament,
        Wherein she sacrificeth, for her part;
        The robes, looks, deeds, desires and whole descent
        Of female natures, built in shops of art,
    Virtue is both the merit and reward
    Of her remov'd, and soul-infus'd regard.

5   Of her remov'd, and soul-infus'd regard,
        With whose firm species (as with golden lances)

    She points her life's field, (for all wars prepar'd)
    And bears one chanceless mind, in all mischances;
Th'invers'd world that goes upon her head
    And with her wanton heels doth kick the sky,
    My love disdains, though she be honoured
    And without envy sees her empery,
Loathes all her toys, and thoughts cupidinine,
    Arranging in the army of her face
    All virtue's forces, to dismay loose eyne
    That hold no quarter with renown, or grace,
War to all frailty; peace of all things pure
Her look doth promise and her life assure.

6   Her look doth promise and her life assure;
    A right line, forcing a rebateless point,
    In her high deeds, through everything obscure
    To full perfection; not the weak disjoint
Of female humours; nor the Protean rages
    Of pied fac'd fashion, that doth shrink and swell,
    Working poor men like waxen images
    And makes them apish strangers where they dwell
Can alter her; titles of primacy,
    Courtship of antic gestures, brainless jests,
    Blood without soul of false nobility,
    Nor any folly that the world infests
Can alter her who with her constant guises
To living virtues turns the deadly vices.

7   To living virtues turns the deadly vices,
    For covetous she is, of all good parts,
    Incontinent for still she shows entices
    To consort with them sucking out their hearts,
Proud, for she scorns prostrate humility,
    And gluttonous in store of abstinence,
    Drunk, with extractions still'd in fervency
    From contemplation, and true continence,
Burning in wrath, against impatience,

       And sloth itself, for she will never rise
          From that all-seeing trance (the band of sense)
          Wherein in view of all soul's skills she lies.
    No constancy to that her mind doth move
    Nor riches to the virtues of my love.

8   Nor riches, to the virtues of my love
        Nor empire to her mighty government:
        Which fair analys'd in her beauty's grove,
        Shows laws for care, and canons for content:
    And as a purple tincture given to glass
        By clear transmission of the sun doth taint
        Opposed subjects: so my Mistress's face
        Doth reverence in her viewer's brows depaint,
    And like the pansy, with a little veil
        She gives her inward work the greater grace;
        Which my lines imitate, though much they fail
        Her gifts so high, and time's conceits so base:
    Her virtues then above my verse must raise her,
    For words want art, and art wants words to praise her.

9   For words want art, and art wants words to praise her,
        Yet shall my active and industrious pen,
        Wind his sharp forehead, through those parts that raise her,
        And register her worth past rarest women.
    Her self shall be my Muse; that well will know
        Her proper inspirations. and assuage
        (With her dear love) the wrongs my fortunes show,
        Which to my youth, bind heartless grief in age,
    Her self shall be my comfort and my riches,
        And all my thoughts I will on her convert,
        Honour, and error, which the world bewitches,
        Shall still crown fools, and tread upon desert,
    And never shall my friendless verse envy
    Muses that fame's loose feathers beautify.

10   Muses that fame's loose feathers beautify,
        And such as scorn to tread the theatre,
        As ignorant: the seed of memory
        Have most inspir'd, and shown their glories there
    To noblest wits, and men of highest doom,
        That for the kingly laurel bent affair;
        The theatres of Athens and of Rome
        Have been the crowns, and not the base impair.
    Far then be this foul cloudy-brow'd contempt
        From like-plum'd birds: and let your sacred rhymes
        From honour's court their servile feet exempt
        That live by soothing moods, and serving times:
    And let my love, adorne with modest eyes,
    Muses that sing love's sensual emperies.

                              Lucidius olim.

DE GUIANA, CARMEN EPICUM
Verses prefixed to
A Relation of the Second Voyage to Guiana
by Laurence Keymis

What work of honour and eternal name,
For all the world t'envy and us t'achieve,
Fills me with furie, and gives armed hands
To my heart's peace, that else would gladly turn
My limbs and every sense into my thoughts
Rapt with the thirsted action of my mind?
O Clio, honour's Muse, sing in my voice,
Tell the attempt, and prophesy th'exploit
Of his Eliza-consecrated sword,
That in this peaceful charm of England's sleep,
Opens most tenderly her aged throat,
Offering to pour fresh youth through all her veins,
That flesh of brass, and ribs of steel retains.

Riches, and conquest, and renown I sing,
Riches with honour, conquest without blood,
Enough to seat the monarchy of earth,
Like to Jove's eagle, on Eliza's hand.
Guiana, whose rich feet are mines of gold,
Whose forehead knocks against the roof of stars,
Stands on her tip-toes at fair England looking,
Kissing her hand, bowing her mighty breast,
And every sign of all submission making,
To be her sister, and the daughter both
Of our most sacred Maid: whose barrenness
Is the true fruit of virtue, that may get,
Bear and bring forth anew in all perfection,
What heretofore savage corruption held
In barbarous chaos; and in this affair
Become her father, mother, and her heir.

Then most admired Sovereign, let your breath
Go forth upon the waters, and create
A golden world in this our iron age,
And be the prosperous forewind to a fleet,
That seconding your last, may go before it
In all success of profit and renown:
Doubt not but your election was divine,
(As well by fate as your high judgement ord'red)
To raise him with choice bounties, that could add
Height to his height; and like a liberal vine,
Not only bear his virtuous fruit aloft,
Free from the press of squint-eyed envy's feet,
But deck his gracious prop with golden bunches,
And shroud it with broad leaves of rule o'ergrown
From all black tempests of invasion.

Those conquests that like general earthquakes shook
The solid world, and made it fall before them,
Built all their brave attempts on weaker grounds,
And less persuasive likelihoods than this;

Nor was there ever princely fount so long
Pour'd forth a sea of rule with so free course,
And such ascending majesty as you:
Then be not like a rough and violent wind,
That in the morning rends the forests down,
Shoves up the seas to heaven, makes earth to tremble,
And tombs his wasteful bravery in the even:
But as a river from a mountain running,
The further he extends, the greater grows,
And by his thrifty race strengthens his stream,
Even to join battle with th'imperious sea
Disdaining his repulse, and in despite
Of his proud fury, mixeth with his main,
Taking on him his titles and commands:
So let thy sovereign empire be increas'd,
And with Iberian Neptune part the stake,
Whose trident he the triple world would make.
You then that would be wise in wisdom's spite,
Directing with discredit of direction,
And hunt for honour, hunting him to death,
With whom before you will inherit gold,
You will lose gold, for which you lose your souls;
You that choose nought for right, but certainty,
And fear that value will get only blows,
Placing your faith in incredulity;
Sit till you see a wonder, virtue rich:
Till honour having gold, rob gold of honour;
Till as men hate desert that getteth nought,
They loathe all getting that deserves not aught,
And use you gold-made men, as dregs of men;
And till your poison'd souls, like spiders lurking
In sluttish chinks, in mists of cobwebs hide
Your foggy bodies, and your dunghill pride.

O incredulity, the wit of fools,
That slovenly will spit on all things fair,

The coward's castle, and the sluggard's cradle,
How easy 'tis to be an infidel!

But you patrician spirits that refine
Your flesh to fire, and issue like a flame
On brave endeavours, knowing that in them
The tract of heaven in morn-like glory opens,
That know you cannot be the kings of earth,
(Claiming the rights of your creation)
And let the mines of earth be kings of you;
That are so far from doubting likely drifts,
That in things hardest y'are most confident;
You that know death lives, where power lives unus'd,
Joying to shine in waves that bury you,
And so make way for life even through your graves;
That will not be content like horse to hold
A thread-bare beaten way to home affairs:
But where the sea in envy of your reign,
Closeth her womb, as fast as 'tis disclos'd,
That she like avarice might swallow all,
And let none find right passage through her rage:
There your wise souls as swift as Eurus lead
Your bodies through, to profit and renown,
And scorn to let your bodies choke your souls,
In the rude breath and prisoned life of beasts:
You that herein renounce the course of earth,
And lift your eyes for guidance to the stars,
That live not for your selves, but to possess
Your honour'd country of a general store;
In pity of the spoil rude self-love makes,
Of them whose lives and yours one air doth feed,
One soil doth nourish, and one strength combine;
You that are blest with sense of all things noble
In this attempt your complete worths redouble.

But how is nature at her heart corrupted,
(I mean even in her most ennobled birth?)

How in excess of sense is sense bereft her!
That her most lightning-like effects of lust
Wound through her flesh, her soul, her flesh unwounded;
And she must need incitements to her good,
Even from that part she hurts. O how most like
Art thou (heroic author of this act)
To this wrong'd soul of nature: that sustain'st
Pain, charge, and peril for thy country's good,
And she much like a body numb'd with surfeits,
Feels not thy gentle applications
For the health, use, and honour of her powers.
Yet shall my verse through all her ease-lock'd ears
Trumpet the noblesse of thy high intent,
And if it cannot into act proceed,
The fault and bitter penance of the fault
Make red some other's eyes with penitence,
For thine are clear; and what more nimble spirits
Apter to bite at such unhooked baits,
Gain by our loss; that must we needs confess
Thy princely valour would have purchas'd us.
Which shall be fame eternal to thy name,
Though thy contentment in thy grave desires,
Of our advancement, fail deserv'd effect,
O how I fear thy glory which I love,
Lest it should dearly grow by our decrease.
Natures that stick in golden-gravell'd springs,
In muck-pits cannot scape their swallowings.

But we shall forth I know; gold is our fate,
Which all our acts doth fashion and create.

Then in the Thespiad's bright prophetic fount,
Methinks I see our Liege rise from her throne,
Her ears and thoughts in steep amaze erected,
At the most rare endeavour of her power.
And now she blesseth with her wonted graces
Th'industrious knight, the soul of this exploit,

Dismissing him to convoy of his stars.
And now for love and honour of his worth,
Our twice-born nobles bring him bridegroom-like,
That is espous'd for virtue to his love
With feasts and music, ravishing the air,
To his Argolian fleet, where round about
His bating colours English valour swarms
In haste, as if Guianian Orenoque
With his fell waters fell upon our shore.
And now a wind as forward as their spirits,
Sets their glad feet on smooth Guiana's breast,
Where (as if each man were an Orpheus)
A world of savages fall tame before them,
Storing their theft-free treasuries with gold,
And there doth plenty crown their wealthy fields,
There learning eats no more his thriftless books,
Nor valour ostrich-like his iron arms.
There beauty is no strumpet for her wants,
Nor gallic humours putrify her blood:
But all our youth take Hymen's lights in hand,
And fill each roof with honour'd progeny.
There makes society adamantine chains,
And joins their hearts with wealth, whom wealth disjoin'd.
There healthful recreations strew their meads,
And make their mansions dance with neighbourhood,
That here were drown'd in churlish avarice.
And there do palaces and temples rise
Out of the earth, and kiss th'enamour'd skies,
Where new Britannia humbly kneels to heaven,
The world to her, and both at her blest feet,
In whom the circles of all empire meet.

HERO AND LEANDER
The Third Sestiad

The Argument

Leander to the envious light
Resigns his night-sports with the night,
And swims the Hellespont again;
Thesme the deity sovereign
Of customs and religious rites
Appears, reproving his delights
Since nuptial honours he neglected;
Which straight he vows shall be effected.
Fair Hero left devirginate
Weighs, and with fury wails her state:
But with her love and woman's wit
She argues, and approveth it.

New light gives new directions, fortunes new
To fashion our endeavours that ensue,
More harsh (at least more hard) more grave and high
Our subject runs, and our stern Muse must fly.
Love's edge is taken off, and that light flame,
Those thoughts, joys, longings, that before became
High unexperienc'd blood, and maids' sharp plights,
Must now grow staid, and censure the delights,
That being enjoy'd ask judgement; now we praise,
As having parted: evenings crown the days.

   And now ye wanton loves, and young desires,
Pied vanity, the mint of strange attires;
Ye lisping flatteries, and obsequious glances,
Relentful musics, and attractive dances,
And you detested charms constraining love,
Shun love's stol'n sports by that these lovers prove.

   By this the sovereign of heaven's golden fires,
And young Leander, lord of his desires,
Together from their lovers' arms arose:
Leander into Hellespontus throws

His Hero-handl'd body, whose delight
Made him disdain each other epithite.
And as amidst the enamoured waves he swims,
The god of gold of purpose gilt his limbs,
That this word gilt, including double sense,
The double guilt of his incontinence,
Might be express'd, that had no stay t'employ
The treasure which the Love-god let him joy
In his dear Hero, with such sacred thrift,
As had beseem'd so sanctified a gift:
But like a greedy vulgar prodigal
Would of the stock dispend, and rudely fall
Before his time, to that unblessed blessing,
Which for lust's plague doth perish with possessing.
   Joy graven in sense, like snow in water wastes;
   Without preserve of virtue nothing lasts.
What man is he that with a wealthy eye
Enjoys a beauty richer than the sky,
Through whose white skin, softer than soundest sleep,
With damask eyes, the ruby blood doth peep,
And runs in branches through her azure veins,
Whose mixture and first fire, his love attains;
Whose both hands limit, both love's deities,
And sweeten human thoughts like paradise;
Whose disposition silken is and kind,
Directed with an earth-exempted mind;
Who thinks not heaven with such a love is given?
And who like earth would spend that dower of heaven,
With rank desire to joy it all at first?
What simply kills our hunger, quencheth thirst,
Clothes but our nakedness, and makes us live,
Praise doth not any of her favours give:
But what doth plentifully minister
Beauteous apparel and delicious cheer,
So ordered that it still excites desire,
And still gives pleasure freeness to aspire,
The palm of bounty ever moist preserving:

To love's sweet life this is the courtly carving.
Thus time, and all-states-ordering Ceremony
Had banish'd all offense: time's golden thigh
Upholds the flowery body of the earth,
In sacred harmony, and every birth
Of men, and actions makes legitimate,
Being us'd aright; *the use of time is fate*.

   Yet did the gentle flood transfer once more
This prize of love home to his father's shore;
Where he unlades himself of that false wealth
That makes few rich; treasures compos'd by stealth;
And to his sister kind Hermione,
(Who on the shore kneel'd, praying to the sea
For his return) he all love's goods did show
In Hero seiz'd for him, in him for Hero.

   His most kind sister all his secrets knew,
And to her singing like a shower he flew,
Sprinkling the earth, that to their tombs took in
Streams dead for love, to leave his ivory skin,
Which yet a snowy foam did leave above,
As soul to the dead water that did love;
And from thence did the first white roses spring,
(For love is sweet and fair in every thing)
And all the sweeten'd shore as he did go,
Was crown'd with od'rous roses white as snow.
Love-bless'd Leander was with love so filled
That love to all that touch'd him he instilled.
And as the colours of all things we see,
To our sight's powers communicated be:
So to all objects that in compass came
Of any sense he had; his senses' flame
Flow'd from his parts, with force so virtual,
It fir'd with sense things mere insensual.

   Now (with warm baths and odours comforted)
When he lay down he kindly kiss'd his bed,
As consecrating it to Hero's right,
And vow'd thereafter that whatever sight

Put him in mind of Hero, or her bliss,
Should be her altar to prefer a kiss.

   Then laid he forth his late enriched arms,
In whose white circle love writ all his charms,
And made his characters sweet Hero's limbs,
When on his breast's warm sea she sideling swims.
And as those arms (held up in circle) met,
He said: See sister Hero's carcanet,
Which she had rather wear about her neck,
Than all the jewels that doth Juno deck.

   But as he shook with passionate desire,
To put in flame his other secret fire,
A music so divine did pierce his ear,
As never yet his ravish'd sense did hear:
When suddenly a light of twenty hues
Brake through the roof, and like the rainbow views
Amaz'd Leander; in whose beams came down
The goddess Ceremony, with a crown
Of all the stars, and heaven with her descended,
Her flaming hair to her bright feet extended,
By which hung all the bench of deities;
And in a chain, compact of ears and eyes,
She led Religion; all her body was
Clear and transparent as the purest glass:
For she was all presented to the sense;
Devotion, Order, State, and Reverence
Her shadows were; Society, Memory;
All which her sight made live; her absence die.
A rich disparent pentacle she wears,
Drawn full of circles and strange characters:
Her face was changeable to every eye;
One way look'd ill, another graciously;
Which while men view'd, they cheerful were and holy:
But looking off, vicious and melancholy:
The snaky paths to each observed law,
Did Policy in her broad bosom draw:
One hand a mathematic crystal sways,

Which gathering in one line a thousand rays
From her bright eyes, Confusion burns to death,
And all estates of men distinguisheth.
By it Morality and Comeliness
Themselves in all their sightly figures dress.
Her other hand a laurel rod applies,
To beat back Barbarism, and Avarice,
That follow'd eating earth, and excrement
And human limbs; and would make proud ascent
To seats of gods, were Ceremony slain;
The Hours and Graces bore her glorious train,
And all the sweets of our society
Were spher'd, and treasur'd in her bounteous eye.
Thus she appear'd, and sharply did reprove
Leander's bluntness in his violent love;
Told him how poor was substance without rites,
Like bills unsign'd, desires without delights;
Like meats unseason'd; like rank corn that grows
On cottages, that none or reaps or sows:
Not being with civil forms confirm'd and bounded,
For human dignities and comforts founded:
But loose and secret all their glories hide,
Fear fills the chamber, darkness decks the bride.

   She vanish'd, leaving pierc'd Leander's heart
With sense of his unceremonious part,
In which with plain neglect of nuptial rites,
He close and flatly fell to his delights:
And instantly he vow'd to celebrate
All rites pertaining to his married state.
So up he gets and to his father goes,
To whose glad ears he doth his vows disclose:
The nuptials are resolv'd with utmost power,
And he at night would swim to Hero's tower.
From whence he meant to Sestos' forked bay
To bring her covertly, where ships must stay,
Sent by his father throughly rigg'd and mann'd,
To waft her safely to Abydos' strand.

There leave we him, and with fresh wing pursue
Astonish'd Hero, whose most wished view
I thus long have forborne, because I left her
So out of countenance, and her spirits bereft her.
To look on one abash'd is impudence,
When of slight faults he hath too deep a sense.
Her blushing het her chamber: she look'd out,
And all the air she purpled round about,
And after it a foul black day befell,
Which ever since a red morn doth foretell:
And still renews our woes for Hero's woe,
And foul it prov'd, because it figur'd so
The next night's horror, which prepare to hear;
I fail if it profane your daintiest ear.

   Then thou most strangely-intellectual fire,
That proper to my soul hast power t'inspire
Her burning faculties, and with the wings
Of thy unsphered flame visit'st the springs
Of spirits immortal; now (as swift as time
Doth follow motion) find th'eternal clime
Of his free soul, whose living subject stood
Up to the chin in the Pierian flood,
And drunk to me half this Musean story,
Inscribing it to deathless memory:
Confer with it, and make my pledge as deep,
That neither's draught be consecrate to sleep.
Tell it how much his late desires I tender,
(If yet it know not) and to light surrender
My soul's dark offspring, willing it should die
To loves, to passions, and society.

   Sweet Hero left upon her bed alone,
Her maidenhead, her vows, Leander gone,
And nothing with her but a violent crew
Of new come thoughts that yet she never knew,
Even to her self a stranger; was much like
Th'Iberian city that war's hand did strike
By English force in princely Essex' guide,

When peace assur'd her towers had fortified;
And golden-finger'd India had bestow'd
Such wealth on her, that strength and empire flow'd
Into her turrets; and her virgin waist
The wealthy girdle of the sea embrac'd:
Till our Leander that made Mars his Cupid,
For soft love-suits, with iron thunders chid:
Swum to her towers, dissolv'd her virgin zone;
Led in his power, and made confusion
Run through her streets amaz'd, that she suppos'd
She had not been in her own walls enclos'd:
But rapt by wonder to some foreign state,
Seeing all her issue so disconsolate:
And all her peaceful mansions possess'd
With war's just spoil, and many a foreign guest
From every corner driving an enjoyer,
Supplying it with power of a destroyer.
So far'd fair Hero in th'expugned fort
Of her chaste bosom, and of every sort
Strange thoughts possess'd her, ransacking her breast
For that that was not there, her wonted rest.
She was a mother straight and bore with pain,
Thoughts that spake straight and wish'd their mother slain;
She hates their lives, and they their own and hers:
Such strife still grows where sin the race prefers.
Love is a golden bubble full of dreams,
That waking breaks, and fills us with extremes.
She mus'd how she could look upon her sire,
And not show that without, that was entire.
For as a glass is an inanimate eye,
And outward forms embraceth inwardly:
So is the eye an animate glass that shows
In-forms without us. And as Phoebus throws
His beams abroad, though he in clouds be clos'd,
Still glancing by them till he find oppos'd,
A loose and rorid vapour that is fit
T'event his searching beams, and useth it

To form a tender twenty-colour'd eye,
Cast in a circle round about the sky:
So when our fiery soul, our body's star,
(That ever is in motion circular)
Conceives a form; in seeking to display it
Through all our cloudy parts, it doth convey it
Forth at the eye, as the most pregnant place,
And that reflects it round about the face.
And this event uncourtly Hero thought,
Her inward guilt would in her looks have wrought:
For yet the world's stale cunning she resisted
To bear foul thoughts, yet forge what looks she listed,
And held it for a very silly sleight,
To make a perfect metal counterfeit:
Glad to disclaim herself, proud of an art,
That makes the face a Pandar to the heart.
Those be the painted moons, whose lights profane
Beauty's true heaven, at full still in their wane.
Those be the lapwing faces that still cry,
Here 'tis, when that they vow is nothing nigh.
Base fools, when every moorish fowl can teach
That which men think the height of human reach.
But custom that the apoplexy is
Of bedrid nature, and lives led amiss,
And takes away all feeling of offense,
Yet braz'd not Hero's brow with impudence;
And this she thought most hard to bring to pass,
To seem in count'nance other than she was,
As if she had two souls; one for the face,
One for the heart; and that they shifted place
As either list to utter, or conceal
What they conceiv'd: or as one soul did deal
With both affairs at once, keeps and ejects
Both at an instant contrary effects:
Retention and ejection in her powers
Being acts alike: for this one vice of ours,
That forms the thought, and sways the countenance,

Rules both our motion and our utterance.
   These and more grave conceits toil'd Hero's spirits:
For though the light of her discursive wits,
Perhaps might find some little hole to pass
Through all these worldly cinctures; yet (alas)
There was a heavenly flame encompass'd her;
Her goddess, in whose fane she did prefer
Her virgin vows; from whose impulsive sight
She knew the black shield of the darkest night
Could not defend her, nor wit's subtlest art:
This was the point pierc'd Hero to the heart.
Who heavy to the death, with a deep sigh
And hand that languish'd, took a robe was nigh,
Exceeding large, and of black Cyprus made,
In which she sat, hid from the day in shade,
Even over head and face down to her feet;
Her left hand made it at her bosom meet;
Her right hand lean'd on her heart-bowing knee,
Wrapp'd in unshapeful folds: 'twas death to see:
Her knee stay'd that, and that her falling face,
Each limb help'd other to put on disgrace.
No form was seen, where form held all her sight:
But like an embryo that saw never light:
Or like a scorched statue made a coal
With three-wing'd lightning: or a wretched soul
Muffl'd with endless darkness, she did sit:
The night had never such a heavy spirit.
Yet might an imitating eye well see,
How fast her clear tears melted on her knee
Through her black veil, and turn'd as black as it,
Mourning to be her tears: then wrought her wit
With her broke vow, her goddess' wrath, her fame,
All tools that enginous despair could frame:
Which made her strew the floor with her torn hair,
And spread her mantle piece-meal in the air.
Like Jove's son's club, strong passion struck her down,
And with a piteous shriek enforc'd her swoon:

Her shriek, made with another shriek ascend
The frighted matron that on her did tend:
And as with her own cry her sense was slain,
So with the other it was call'd again.
She rose and to her bed made forced way,
And laid her down even where Leander lay:
And all this while the red sea of her blood,
Ebb'd with Leander: but now turn'd the flood
And all her fleet of sprites came swelling in
With child of sail, and did hot fight begin
With those severe conceits, she too much mark'd,
And here Leander's beauties were embark'd.
He came in swimming painted all with joys,
Such as might sweeten hell: his thought destroys
All her destroying thoughts: she thought she felt
His heart in hers with her contentions melt,
And chid her soul that it could so much err,
To check the true joys he deserv'd in her.
Her fresh heat blood cast figures in her eyes,
And she suppos'd she saw in Neptune's skies
How her star wander'd, wash'd in smarting brine
For her love's sake, that with immortal wine
Should be embath'd, and swim in more heart's ease,
Than there was water in the Sestian seas.
Then said her Cupid-prompted spirit: Shall I
Sing moans to such delightsome harmony?
Shall slick-tongu'd Fame patch'd up with voices rude,
The drunken bastard of the multitude,
(Begot when father Judgement is away,
And gossip-like, says because others say,
Takes news as if it were too hot to eat,
And spits it slavering forth for dog-fees meat)
Make me for forging a fantastic vow,
Presume to bear what makes grave matrons bow?
Good vows are never broken with good deeds,
For then good deeds were bad: vows are but seeds,
And good deeds fruits; even those good deeds that grow
From other stocks, than from th'observed vow.

53

That is a good deed that prevents a bad:
Had I not yielded, slain myself I had.
Hero Leander is, Leander Hero:
Such virtue love hath to make one of two.
If then Leander did my maidenhead get,
Leander being myself I still retain it.
We break chaste vows when we live loosely ever:
But bound as we are, we live loosely never.
Two constant lovers being join'd in one,
Yielding to one another, yield to none.
We know not how to vow, till love unblind us,
And vows made ignorantly never bind us.
Too true it is that when 'tis gone men hate
The joys as vain they took in love's estate:
But that's since they have lost the heavenly light
Should show them way to judge of all things right.
When life is gone death must implant his terror,
As death is foe to life, so love to error.
Before we love how range we through this sphere,
Searching the sundry fancies hunted here:
Now with desire of wealth transported quite
Beyond our free humanity's delight:
Now with ambition climbing falling towers,
Whose hope to scale our fear to fall devours:
Now rapt with pastimes, pomp, all joys impure;
In things without us no delight is sure.
But love with all joys crown'd, within doth sit;
O Goddess pity love and pardon it.
This spake she weeping: but her goddess' ear
Burn'd with too stern a heat, and would not hear.
Ay me, hath heaven's straight fingers no more graces,
For such as Hero, than for homeliest faces?
Yet she hop'd well, and in her sweet conceit
Weighing her arguments, she thought them weight:
And that the logic of Leander's beauty,
And them together would bring proofs of duty.
And if her soul, that was a skilful glance

Of heaven's great essence, found such imperance
In her love's beauties; she had confidence
Jove lov'd him too, and pardon'd her offense.
Beauty in heaven and earth this grace doth win,
It supples rigour, and it lessens sin.
Thus, her sharp wit, her love, her secrecy,
Trouping together, made her wonder why
She should not leave her bed, and to the temple?
Her health said she must live; her sex, dissemble.
She view'd Leander's place, and wish'd he were
Turn'd to his place, so his place were Leander.
Aye me (said she) that love's sweet life and sense
Should do it harm! my love had not gone hence,
Had he been like his place. O blessed place,
Image of constancy. Thus my love's grace
Parts no where but it leaves some thing behind
Worth observation: he renowns his kind.
His motion is like heaven's orbicular:
For where he once is, he is ever there.
This place was mine: Leander now 'tis thine;
Thou being myself, then it is double mine:
Mine, and Leander's mine, Leander's mine.
O see what wealth it yields me, nay yields him:
For I am in it, he for me doth swim.
Rich, fruitful love, that doubling self estates
Elixir-like contracts, though separates.
Dear place I kiss thee, and do welcome thee,
As from Leander ever sent to me.

from the *Fifth Sestiad* [lines 427-480]

from The Argument

... *[Hero] makes a feast, at which appears*
The wild nymph Teras, that still bears
An ivory lute, tells ominous tales
And sings at solemn festivals.

Epithalamion Teratos

Come, come dear night, love's mart of kisses,
Sweet close of his ambitious line,
The fruitful summer of his blisses,
Love's glory doth in darkness shine.
O come soft rest of cares, come night,
Come naked virtue's only tire,
The reaped harvest of the light,
Bound up in sheaves of sacred fire.
    Love calls to war,
    Sighs his alarms,
    Lips his swords are,
    The field his arms.
Come night and lay thy velvet hand
On glorious day's outfacing face;
And all thy crowned flames command,
For torches to our nuptial grace.
    Love calls to war,
    Sighs his alarms,
    Lips his swords are,
    The field his arms.
No need have we of factious day,
To cast in envy of thy peace,
Her balls of discord in thy way:
Here beauty's day doth never cease,
Day is abstracted here,
And varied in a triple sphere.
Hero, Alcmane, Mya, so outshine thee,
Ere thou come here let Thetis thrice refine thee.

> *Love calls to war,*
> *Sighs his alarms,*
> *Lips his swords are,*
> *The field his arms.*

The evening star I see:
Rise youths, the evening star,
Helps love to summon war,
Both now embracing be.
Rise youths, love's right claims more than banquets, rise.
Now the bright marigolds that deck the skies,
Phoebus' celestial flow'rs, that (contrary
To his flowers here) ope when he shuts his eye,
And shuts when he doth open, crown your sports:
Now love in night, and night in love exhorts
Courtship and dances: all your parts employ,
And suit night's rich expansure with your joy,
Love paints his longings in sweet virgins' eyes:
Rise youths, love's right claims more than banquets, rise.
Rise virgins, let fair nuptial loves enfold
Your fruitless breasts: the maidenheads ye hold
Are not your own alone, but parted are;
Part in disposing them your parents share,
And that a third part is: so must ye save
Your loves a third, and you your thirds must have.
Love paints his longings in sweet virgins' eyes:
Rise youths, love's right claims more than banquets, rise.

PERISTEROS. OR THE MALE TURTLE

Not like that loose and party-liver'd sect
    Of idle lovers, that (as different lights,
On colour'd subjects, different hues reflect;)
    Change their affections with their mistress' sights,
That with her praise, or dispraise, drown, or float,
    And must be fed with fresh conceits, and fashions;
Never wax cold, but die: love not, but dote:

'(Love's fires, staid judgements blow, not humorous
                                                passions,)
Whose loves upon their lovers' pomp depend,
    And quench as fast as her eyes sparkle twinkles,
'(Nought lasts that doth to outward worth contend,
    All love in smooth brows born is tomb'd in wrinkles.)'
But like the consecrated bird of love,
    Whose whole life's hap to his soul-mate alluded,
Whom no proud flocks of other fowls could move,
    But in herself all company concluded.
She was to him th'analysed world of pleasure,
    Her firmness cloth'd him in variety;
Excess of all things, he joy'd in her measure,
    Mourn'd when she mourn'd, and dieth when she dies,
Like him I bound th'instinct of all my powers,
    In her that bounds the empire of desert,
And time nor change (that all things else devours,
    But truth eterniz'd in a constant heart)
Can change me more from her, than her from merit,
That is my form, and gives my being, spirit.

from EUTHYMIAE RAPTUS
or The Tears of Peace

To the high-born Prince of men, Henry, thrice-royal inheritor to the United Kingdoms of Great Britain

Inductio

Now that our sovereign, the great King of Peace
Hath (in her grace) outlabour'd Hercules;
And, past his pillars, stretch'd her victories;
Since (as he were sole soul, t'all royalties)
He moves all kings, in this vast universe,
To cast chaste nets on th'impious lust of Mars;
See, all; and imitate his goodness still;
That (having clear'd so well, war's outward ill)

He, god-like, still employs his firm desires,
To cast learn'd ink upon those inward fires,
That kindle worse war, in the minds of men,
Like to incense the outward war again:
Self-love, inflaming so, men's sensual blood,
That all good, public, drowns in private good;
And that, sinks under, his own over-freight;
Men's reasons, and their learnings, shipwrack'd quite;
And their religion, that should still be one,
Take shapes so many, that most know't in none.
Which, I admiring (since, in each man shin'd
A light so clear, that by it, all might find
(Being well inform'd) their object perfect peace,
Which keeps the narrow path to happiness)
In that discourse; I shunn'd, (as is my use)
The jarring preace, and all their time's abuse;
T'enjoy least trodden fields, and free'st shades;
Wherein (of all the pleasure that invades
The life of man, and flies all vulgar feet,
Since silent meditation is most sweet)
I sat to it; discoursing what main want
So ransack'd man; that it did quite supplant
The inward peace I spake of; letting in
(At his loose veins) sad war, and all his sin.
When, suddenly, a comfortable light
Brake through the shade; and, after it, the sight
Of a most grave, and goodly person shin'd;
With eyes turn'd upwards, and was outward, blind;
But, inward; past, and future things, he saw;
And was to both, and present times, their law.
His sacred bosom was so full of fire,
That 'twas transparent; and made him expire
His breath in flames, that did instruct (methought)
And (as my soul were then at full) they wrought.
At which, I casting down my humble eyes,
Not daring to attempt their fervencies;
He thus bespake me; Dear mind, do not fear

My strange appearance; now 'tis time t'outwear
Thy bashful disposition, and put on
As confident a count'nance, as the sun.
For what hast thou to look on, more divine,
And horrid, than man is; as he should shine,
And as he doth? what, freed from this world's strife;
What he is ent'ring; and what, ending life?
All which, thou only studiest, and dost know;
And, more than which, is only sought for show.
Thou must not undervalue what thou hast,
In weighing it with that, which more is grac'd;
The worth that weigheth inward, should not long
For outward prices. This should make thee strong
In thy close value; nought so good can be
As that which lasts good, betwixt God, and thee.
Remember thine own verse—Should heaven turn hell,
For deeds well done, I would do ever well.

    This heard, with joy enough, to break the twin
Of life and soul, so apt to break as mine;
I brake into a trance, and then remain'd
(Like him) an only soul; and so obtain'd
Such boldness, by the sense he did control;
That I set look, to look; and soul to soul.
I view'd him at his brightest; though, alas,
With all acknowledgement, of what he was
Beyond what I found habited in me;
And thus I spake; O thou that (blind) dost see
My heart, and soul; what may I reckon thee?
Whose heavenly look shows not; nor voice sounds man?
I am (said he) that spirit Elysian,
That (in thy native air; and on the hill
Next Hitchin's left hand) did thy bosom fill,
With such a flood of soul; that thou wert fain
(With acclamations of her rapture then)
To vent it, to the echoes of the vale;
When (meditating of me) a sweet gale
Brought me upon thee; and thou did'st inherit

My true sense (for the time then) in my spirit;
And I, invisibly, went prompting thee,
To those fair greens, where thou did'st english me.

    Scarce he had utter'd this, when well I knew
It was my prince's Homer; whose dear view
Renew'd my grateful memory of the grace
His highness did me for him: which, in face,
Me thought the spirit show'd, was his delight;
And added glory to his heavenly plight:
Who told me, he brought stay to all my state;
That he was angel to me; star, and fate;
Advancing colours of good hope to me;
And told me, my retired age should see
Heaven's blessing, in a free, and harmless life,
Conduct me, through earth's peace-pretending strife,
To that true peace, whose search I still intend,
And to the calm shore of a loved end.

    But now, as I cast round my ravish'd eye,
To see, if this free soul had company;
Or that, alone, he lovingly pursued
The hidden places of my solitude;
He rent a cloud down, with his burning hand
That at his back hung, 'twixt me, and a land
Never inhabited; and said; Now, behold
What main defect it is that doth enfold
The world, in ominous flatteries of a peace
So full of worse than war; whose stern increase
Devours her issue. With which words, I view'd
A lady, like a deity endu'd;
(But weeping, like a woman) and made way
Out of one thicket, that saw never day,
Towards another; bearing underneath
Her arm, a coffin, for some prize of death;
And after her (in funeral form) did go
The wood's four-footed beasts, by two, and two;
A male, and female, match'd, of every kind;
And after them; with like instinct inclin'd,

The airy nation felt her sorrow's stings;
Fell on the earth, kept rank, and hung their wings.
Which sight I much did pity, and admire;
And long'd to know the dame that could inspire
Those bestials, with such human form, and ruth;
And how I now should know, the hidden truth
(As Homer promis'd) of that main defect
That makes men, all their inward peace reject
For name of outward: then he took my hand;
Led to her; and would make myself demand,
(Though he could have resolv'd me) what she was?
And from what cause, those strange effects had pass?
For whom, she bore that coffin? and so mourn'd?
To all which; with all mildness, she return'd
Answer; that she was Peace; sent down from heaven
With charge, from the almighty Deity given,
T'attend on men; who now had banish'd her
From their societies, and made her err
In that wild desert; only Human Love
(Banish'd in like sort) did a long time prove
That life with her; but now, alas, was dead,
And lay in that wood to be buried;
For whom she bore that coffin, and did mourn;
And that those beasts were so much human, born,
That they, in nature, felt a love to peace;
For which, they follow'd her, when men did cease.
This went so near her heart, it left her tongue;
And (silent) she gave time, to note whence sprung
Men's want of peace, which was from want of love:
And I observ'd now, what that peace did prove
That men made shift with, and did so much please.
For now, the sun declining to the seas,
Made long misshapen shadows; and true peace
(Here walking in his beams) cast such increase
Of shadow from her; that I saw it glide
Through cities, courts, and countries; and descried,
How, in her shadow only, men there liv'd,

While she walk'd here i'th'sun: and all that thriv'd
Hid in that shade their thrift; nought but her shade
Was bulwark 'gainst all war that might invade
Their countries, or their consciences; since love
(That should give peace, her substance) now they drove
Into the deserts; where he suffered fate,
And whose sad funerals beasts must celebrate.
With whom, I freely wish'd, I had been nurs'd;
Because they follow nature, at their worst;
And at their best, did teach her. As we went
I felt a scruple, which I durst not vent,
No not to peace herself, whom it concern'd,
For fear to wrong her; so well I have learn'd,
To shun injustice, even to doves, or flies;
But, to the devil, or the destinies,
Where I am just, and know I honour truth,
I'll speak my thoughts, in scorn of what ensu'th.
Yet (not resolv'd in th'other) there did shine
A beam of Homer's freer soul, in mine,
That made me see, I might propose my doubt;
Which was; if this were true peace I found out,
That felt such passion? I prov'd her sad part;
And pray'd her call, her voice out of her heart
(There, kept a wrongful prisoner to her woe)
To answer, why she was afflicted so.
Or how, in her, such contraries could fall;
That taught all joy, and was the life of all?
She answer'd; Homer told me that there are
Passions, in which corruption hath no share;
There is a joy of soul; and why not then
A grief of soul, that is no scathe to men?
For both are passions, though not such as reign
In blood, and humour, that engender pain.
Free sufferance for the truth, makes sorrow sing,
And mourning far more sweet, than banqueting.
Good, that deserveth joy (receiving ill)
Doth merit justly, as much sorrow still:

And is it a corruption to do right?
Grief, that dischargeth conscience, is delight:
One sets the other off. To stand at gaze
In one position, is a stupid maze,
Fit for a statue. This resolv'd me well,
That grief, in peace, and peace in grief might dwell.
    And now fell all things from their natural birth:
Passion in heaven; stupidity, in earth,
Inverted all; the muses, virtues, graces,
Now suffer'd rude, and miserable chases
From men's societies, to that desert heath;
And after them, religion (chas'd by death)
Came weeping, bleeding to the funeral:
Sought her dear mother peace; and down did fall,
Before her, fainting, on her horned knees;
Turn'd horn, with praying for the miseries
She left the world in; desperate in their sin;
Marble, her knees pierc'd; but heaven could not win
To stay the weighty ruin of his glory
In her sad exile; all the memory
Of heaven and heavenly things, raz'd of all hands;
Heaven moves so far off that men say it stands;
And earth is turn'd the true and moving heaven;
And so 'tis left; and so is all truth driven
From her false bosom; all is left alone,
Till all be order'd with confusion.
Thus the poor brood of peace, driven and distrest,
Lay brooded all beneath their mother's breast;
Who fell upon them weeping, as they fell:
All were so pin'd, that she contain'd them well.
And in this chaos, the digestion
And beauty of the world, lay thrust and thrown.
In this dejection peace pour'd out her tears,
Worded, (with some pause) in my wounded ears.

       [*Invocatio,* lines 228-65 omitted]

The Tears of Peace

Thou wretched man, whom I discover, born   *Peace*
To want, and sorrow, and the vulgar's scorn:
Why haunt'st thou freely, these unhaunted places,
Empty of pleasure? empty of all graces,
Fashions, and riches; by the best pursu'd
With broken sleep, toil, love, zeal, servitude;
With fear and trembling, with whole lives, and souls?
While thou break'st sleeps, digg'st under earth, like moles,
To live, to seek me out, whom all men fly:
And think'st to find, light in obscurity,
Eternity, in this deep vale of death:
Look'st ever upwards, and liv'st still beneath;
Fill'st all thy actions, with strife, what to think,
Thy brain with air, and scatter'st it in ink:
Of which thou mak'st weeds for thy soul to wear,
As out of fashion, as the bodies are.
I grant their strangeness, and their too ill grace,   *Interlo.*
And too much wretchedness, to bear the face
Or any likeness of my soul in them:
Whose instruments, I rue with many a stream
Of secret tears for their extreme defects,
In uttering her true forms: but their respects
Need not be less'ned, for their being strange,
Or not so vulgar, as the rest that range
With headlong raptures, through the multitude:
Of whom they get grace, for their being rude.
Nought is so shunn'd by virtue, thrown from truth,
As that which draws the vulgar dames, and youth.
Truth must confess it: for where lives there one,   *Peace*
That truth or virtue, for themselves alone,
Or seeks, or not contemns? All, all pursue
Wealth, glory, greatness, pleasure, fashions new.
Who studies, studies these: who studies not
And sees that study, lays the vulgar plot;
That all the learning he gets living by,

Men but for form, or humour dignify
(As himself studies, but for form, and show,
And never makes his special end, to know)
And that an idle, airy man of news,
A standing face; a property to use
In all things vile, makes book-worms, creep to him:
How scorns he books, and book-worms! O how dim
Burns a true soul's light, in his bastard eyes!
And, as a forest over-grown breeds flies,
Toads, adders, savages, that all men shun;
When, on the south-side, in a fresh May sun,
In varied herds, the beasts lie out, and sleep,
The busy gnats, in swarms a buzzing keep,
And gild their empty bodies (lift aloft)
In beams, that though they see all, difference nought:
So, in men's merely outward, and false peace,
Instead of polish'd men, and true increase,
She brings forth men, with vices overgrown,
Women, so light, and like, few know their own:
For mild and human tongues, tongues fork'd that sting:
And all these (while they may) take sun, and spring . . .
                        [lines 322-398 omitted]
If learning then, in love or act must be,   *Interlo.*
Mean to good life, and true humanity;
Where are our scarecrows now, or men of rags,
Of titles merely, places, fortunes, brags,
That want and scorn both? Those inverted men?
Those dungeons; whose souls no more contain
The actual light of reason, than dark beasts?
Those clouds, driven still, twixt God's beam and their breasts?
Those giants, throwing golden hills 'gainst heaven?
To no one spice of true humanity given?
Of men, there are three sorts, that most foes be   *Peace*
To learning and her love; themselves and me:
Active, passive, and intellective men:
Whose self-loves; learning, and her love disdain.
Your active men, consume their whole life's fire,

In thirst of state-height, higher still and higher,
(Like seeled pigeons) mounting, to make sport,
To lower lookers on; in seeing how short
They come of that they seek, and with what trouble;
Lamely, and far from nature, they redouble
Their pains in flying, more than humbler wits,
To reach death, more direct. For death that sits
Upon the fist of fate, past highest air,
(Since she commands all lives, within that sphere)
The higher men advance; the nearer finds
Her seeled quarries; when, in bitterest winds,
Lightnings, and thunders, and in sharpest hails
Fate casts her off at states; when lower sails
Slide calmly to their ends. Your passive men
(So call'd of only passing time in vain)
Pass it, in no good exercise; but are
In meats, and cups laborious; and take care
To lose without all care their soul-spent time;
And since they have no means, nor spirits to climb,
Like fowls of prey, in any high affair;
See how like kites they bangle in the air,
To stoop at scraps, and garbage; in respect,
Of that which men of true peace should select;
And how they trot out, in their lives, the ring;
With idly iterating oft one thing,
A new-fought combat, an affair at sea;
A marriage, or a progress, or a plea.
No news, but fits them, as if made for them,
Though it be forg'd, but of a woman's dream;
And stuff with, such stol'n ends, their manless breasts,
(Sticks, rags, and mud) they seem mere puttocks' nests:
Curious in all men's actions, but their own;
All men, and all things censure, though know none.
Your intellective men, they study hard
Not to get knowledge, but for mere reward.
And therefore that true knowledge that should be
Their studies' end, and is in nature free;

67

Will not be made their broker; having power
(With her sole self) to bring both bride, and dower.
They have some shadows of her (as of me,
Adulterate outward peace) but never see
Her true and heavenly face. Yet those shades serve
(Like errant knights, that by enchantments swerve,
From their true lady's being; and embrace
An ugly witch, with her fantastic face)
To make them think, truth's substance in their arms:
Which that they have not, but her shadow's charms,
See if my proofs, be like their arguments
That leave opinion still, her free dissents.
They have not me with them; that all men know
The highest fruit that doth of knowledge grow;
The bound of all true forms, and only act;
If they be true, they rest; nor can be rackt
Out of their posture, by time's utmost strength;
But last the more of force, the more of length;
For they become one substance with the soul;
Which time with all his adjuncts shall control.
But since, men wilful may believe perchance
(In part of error's two-fold ignorance,
Ill disposition) their skills look as high
And rest in that divine security;
See if their lives make proof of such a peace,
For learning's truth makes all life's vain war cease;
It making peace with God, and joins to God;
Whose information drives her period
Through all the body's passive instruments;
And by reflection gives them soul-contents,
Besides from perfect learning you can never
Wisdom (with her fair reign of passions) sever;
For wisdom is nought else, than learning fin'd,
And with the understanding pow'r combin'd;
That is, a habit of both habits standing;
The blood's vain humours, ever countermanding.
But, if these show, more humour than th'unlearn'd;

If in them more vain passion be discern'd;
More mad ambition; more lust, more deceit;
More show of gold, than gold; than dross, less weight;
If flattery, avarice have their souls so given,
Headlong, and with such devilish furies driven;
That fools may laugh at their imprudency,
And villains blush at their dishonesty;
Where is true learning, prov'd to separate these
And seat all forms in her soul's height, in peace?
Raging Euripus, that (in all their pride)
Drives ships 'gainst roughest winds, with his fierce tide,
And ebbs and flows, seven times in every day;
Toils not on earth with more irregular sway,
Nor is more turbulent, and mad than they.
And shine; like gold-worms, whom you hardly find,
By their own, light; not seen; but heard like wind.
But this is learning; to have skill to throw
Reins on your body's pow'rs, that nothing know;
And fill the soul's powers, so with act, and art,
That she can curb the body's angry part;
All perturbations; all effects that stray
From their one object; which is to obey
Her sovereign empire; as her self should force
Their functions only, to serve her discourse;
And, that; to beat the straight path of one end
Which is, to make her substance still contend,
To be God's image; in informing it,
With knowledge; holy thoughts, and all forms fit
For that eternity, ye seek in way
Of his sole imitation, and to sway,
Your life's love so, that he may still be centre
To all your pleasures; and you, (here) may enter
The next life's peace; in governing so well
Your sensual parts, that you, as free may dwell
Of vulgar raptures, here; as when calm death
Dissolves that learned empire, with your breath.
To teach, and live thus, is the only use,

69

And end of learning, skill that doth produce
But terms, and tongues, and parroting of art,
Without that pow'r to rule the errant part;
Is that which some call, learned ignorance;
A serious trifle; error in a trance.
And let a scholar, all earth's volumes carry,
He will be but a walking dictionary:
A mere articulate clock, that doth but speak
By others' arts; when wheels wear, or springs break,
Or any fault is in him; he can mend
No more than clocks; but at set hours must spend
His mouth, as clocks do; if too fast, speech go
He cannot stay it; nor haste if too slow.
So that, as travellers, seek their peace through storms,
In passing many seas, for many forms,
Of foreign government; endure the pain
Of many faces seeing; and the gain
That strangers make, of their strange-loving humours;
Learn tongues; keep note-books; all to feed the tumours
Of vain discourse at home; or serve the course
Of state employment, never having force
T'employ themselves; but idle complements
Must pay their pains, costs, slaveries, all their rents;
And, though they many men know, get few friends:
So covetous readers; setting many ends
To their much skill to talk; studiers of phrase;
Shifters in art; to flutter in the blaze
Of ignorant count'nance; to obtain degrees
And lie in learning's bottom, like the lees,
To be accounted deep, by shallow men;
And carve all language, in one glorious pen;
May have much fame for learning: but th'effect
Proper to perfect learning; to direct
Reason in such an art, as that it can
Turn blood to soul, and make both, one calm man;
So making peace with God; doth differ far
From clerks that go with God and man to war.

[lines 562-1080 omitted]

Conclusio

Thus, by the way, to human love's interring,
These marginal, and secret tears referring
To my disposure (having all this hour
Of our unworldly conference, given pow'r
To her late-fainting issue, to arise)
She rais'd herself, and them; the progenies
Of that so civil desert, rising all;
Who fell with her; and to the funeral
(She bearing still the coffin) all went on.
And, now gives time, her state's description.
Before her flew affliction, girt in storms,
Gash'd all with gushing wounds; and all the forms
Of bane, and misery, frowning in her face;
Whom tyranny, and injustice, had in chase;
Grim persecution, poverty, and shame;
Detraction, envy, foul mishap and lame;
Scruple of conscience; fear, deceit, despair;
Slander, and clamour, that rent all the air;
Hate, war, and massacre; uncrowned toil;
And sickness (t'all the rest, the base, and foil)
Crept after; and his deadly weight, trod down
Wealth, beauty, and the glory of a crown.
These usher'd her far off; as figures given,
To show, these crosses borne, make peace with heaven:
But now (made free from them) next her, before;
Peaceful, and young, Herculean silence bore
His craggy club; which up, aloft, he held;
With which, and his forefinger's charm he still'd
All sounds in air; and left so free, mine ears,
That I might hear, the music of the spheres,
And all the angels, singing, out of heaven;
Whose tunes were solemn (as to passion given)
For now, that justice was the happiness there
For all the wrongs to right, inflicted here.

Such was the passion that peace now put on;
And on, all went; when suddenly was gone
All light of heaven before us; from a wood
Whose sight, foreseen (now lost) amaz'd we stood,
The sun still gracing us; when now (the air
Inflam'd with meteors) we discover'd, fair,
The skipping goat; the horse's flaming mane;
Bearded, and trained comets; stars in wane;
The burning sword; the firebrand, flying snake;
The lance; the torch; the licking fire; the drake:
And all else Meteors, that did ill abode;
The thunder chid; the lightning leapt abroad;
And yet, when peace came in, all heaven was clear;
And then, did all the horrid wood appear;
Where mortal dangers, more than leaves did grow;
In which we could not, one free step bestow;
For treading on some murder'd passenger,
Who thither, was by witchcraft, forc'd to err,
Whose face, the bird hid, that loves humans best;
That hath the bugle eyes, and rosy breast;
And is the yellow autumn's nightingale.
Peace made us enter here secure of all;
Where, in a cave, that through a rock did eat
The monster, Murder, held his impious seat:
A heap of panting harts, supported him;
On which, he sat, gnawing a reeking limb,
Of some man newly murder'd. As he ate
His grave-digg'd brows, like stormy eaves did sweat;
Which, like incensed fens, with mists did smoke;
His hide was rugged, as an aged oak
With heathy leprosies; that still he fed
With hot, raw limbs, of men late murdered.
His face was like a meteor, flashing blood;
His head all bristl'd, like a thorny wood;
His neck cast wrinkles, like a sea enrag'd;
And, in his vast arms, was the world engag'd,
Bathing his hands in every cruel deed;

Whose palms were hell-deep lakes of boiling lead;
His thighs were mines of poison, torment, grief;
In which digg'd fraud, and treachery, for relief;
Religion's botcher, policy; and pride;
Oppression, slavery, flattery glorified;
Atheism, and tyranny, and gain unjust;
Frantic ambition, envy, shag-hair'd lust;
Both sorts of ignorance; and knowledge swell'd;
And over these, the old wolf avarice held
A golden scourge, that dropp'd, with blood and vapour;
With which, he whipp'd them to their endless labour.
From under heaps, cast from his fruitful thighs,
(As ground, to all their damn'd impieties)
The mournful goddess, drew dead human love;
Nor could they let her entry, though they strove;
And furnac'd on her, all their venomous breath;
(For; though all outrage breaks the peace of death)
She coffin'd him; and forth to funeral
All help'd to bear him: but to sound it all,
My trumpet fails; and all my forces shrink.
Who can enact to life, what kills to think?
Nor can the soul's beams bear, through blood and flesh,
Forms of such woe, and height, as now, afresh,
Flow'd from these objects: to see poesy
Prepar'd to do the special obsequy,
And sing the funeral oration;
How it did show, to see her tread upon
The breast of death; and on a fury lean;
How, to her fist, (as rites of service then)
A cast of ravens flew; on her shoulders, how
The fowls, that to the muses' queen we vow,
(The owl, and heronshaw) sat, how, for her hair,
A hapless comet, hurl'd about the air
Her curled beams: whence sparks, like falling stars.
Vanish'd about her; and with winds adverse,
Were still blown back; to which the phoenix flew;
And (burning on her head) would not renew:

How her divine oration did move,
For th'unredeemed loss of human love;
Object man's future state to reason's eye;
The soul's infusion; immortality;
And prove her forms firm, that are here impress'd;
How her admir'd strains, wrought on every beast;
And made the woods cast their immanity,
Up to the air; that did to cities fly
In fuel for them: and, in clouds of smoke,
Ever hang over them; cannot be spoke;
Nor how to human love (to earth now given)
A lightning stoop'd, and ravish'd him to heaven,
And with him peace, with all her heavenly seed:
Whose outward rapture, made me inward bleed;
Nor can I therefore, my intention keep;
Since tears want words, and words want tears to weep.
    [*Corollarium ad Principem*, lines 1205-1232, omitted]

THE ILIADS OF HOMER
from *To the Reader*

Whom shall we choose the glory of all wits,
    Held through so many sorts of discipline,
And such variety of works, and spirits;
    But Grecian Homer? like whom none did shine,
For form of work and matter. And because
    Our proud doom of him may stand justified
By noblest judgements; and receive applause
    In spite of envy, and illiterate pride;
Great Macedon, amongst his matchless spoils,
    Took from rich Persia (on his fortunes cast)
A casket finding (full of precious oils)
    Form'd all of gold, with wealthy stones enchas'd:
He took the oils out; and his nearest friends
    Ask'd, in what better guard it might be used?
All giving their conceits, to several ends;

    He answer'd; His affections rather choos'd
An use quite opposite to all their kinds:
    And Homer's books should with that guard be serv'd;
That the most precious work of all men's minds,
    In the most precious place, might be preserv'd.
The fount of wit was Homer; learning's sire,
    And gave antiquity, her living fire.

Volumes of like praise, I could heap on this,
    Of men more ancient, and more learn'd than these:
But since true virtue, enough lovely is
    With her own beauties; all the suffrages
Of others I omit; and would more fain
    That Homer, for himself, should be belov'd
Who every sort of love-worth did contain.
    Which now I have in my conversion prov'd.
I must confess, I hardly dare refer
    To reading judgements; since, so generally,
Custom hath made even th'ablest agents err
    In these translations; all so much apply
Their pains and cunnings, word for word to render
    Their patient authors; when they may as well,
Make fish with fowl, camels with whales engender;
    Or their tongues' speech, in other mouths compel.
For, even as different a production
    Ask Greek and English; since as they in sounds,
And letters, shun one form, and unison;
    So have their sense, and elegancy bounds
In their distinguish'd natures, and require
    Only a judgement to make both consent,
In sense and elocution; and aspire
    As well to reach the spirit that was spent
In his example; as with art to pierce
    His grammar, and etymology of words.
But, as great clerks, can write no English verse;
    Becasue (alas! great clerks) English affords
(Say they) no height, nor copy; a rude tongue,

   (Since 'tis their native): but in Greek or Latin
Their wits are rare; for thence true poesy sprung:
   Though them (truth knows) they have but skill to chat in,
Compar'd with that they might say in their own;
   Since thither th'other's full soul cannot make
The ample transmigration to be shown
   In nature-loving poesy: so the brake
That those translators stick in, that affect
   Their word for word traductions (where they lose
The free grace of their natural dialect
   And shame their authors, with a forced gloss)
I laugh to see; and yet as much abhor
   More license from the words, than may express
Their full compression, and make clear the author.
   From whose truth, if you think my feet digress,
Because I use needful periphrases;
   Read Valla, Hessus, that in Latin prose,
And verse convert him; read the Messines,
   That into Tuscan turns him; and the gloss
Grave Salel makes in French, as he translates:
   Which (for th'aforesaid reasons) all must do;
And see that my conversion much abates
   The license they take, and more shows him too:
Whose right, not all those great learn'd men have done
   (In some main parts), that were his commentars:
But (as the illustration of the sun
   Should be attempted by the erring stars)
They fail'd to search his deep, and treasurous heart.
   The cause was, since they wanted the fit key
Of nature, in their down-right strength of art;
   With poesy, to open poesy.
Which in my poem of the mysteries
   Reveal'd in Homer, I will clearly prove;
Till whose near birth, suspend your calumnies,
   And far-wide imputations of self-love.
'Tis further from me, than the worst that reads;
   Professing me the worst of all that write:

Yet what, in following one, that bravely leads,
   The worst may show, let this proof hold the light.
But grant it clear: yet hath detraction got
   My blind side, in the form, my verse puts on;
Much like a dung-hill mastiff, that dares not
   Assault the man he barks at; but the stone
He throws at him, takes in his eager jaws,
   And spoils his teeth because they cannot spoil.
The long verse hath by proof receiv'd applause
   Beyond each number: and the foil,
That squint-ey'd envy takes, is censur'd plain.
   For, this long poem asks this length of verse,
Which I myself ingenuously maintain
   Too long, our shorter authors to rehearse.
And, for our tongue, that still is so impair'd
   By travailing linguists; I can prove it clear,
That no tongue hath the muses' utterance heir'd
   For verse, and that sweet music to the ear
Struck out of rhyme, so naturally, as this;
   Our monosyllables, so kindly fall
And meet, oppos'd in rhyme, as they did kiss:
   French and Italian, most immetrical;
Their many syllables, in harsh collision,
   Fall as they brake their necks; their bastard rhymes,
Saluting as they jostl'd in transition,
   And set our teeth on edge; nor tunes, nor times
Kept in their falls. And methinks, their long words
   Show in short verse, as in a narrow place,
Two opposites should meet, with two-hand swords
   Unwieldily, without or use or grace.
Thus having rid the rubs, and strow'd these flowers
   In our thrice sacred Homer's English way;
What rests to make him, yet more worthy yours?
   To cite more praise of him, were mere delay
To your glad searches, for what those men found,
   That gave his praise, past all, so high a place:
Whose virtues were so many, and so crown'd,

By all consents, divine; that not to grace,
Or add increase to them, the world doth need
    Another Homer; but even to rehearse
And number them: they did so much exceed;
    Men thought him not a man; but that his verse
Some mere celestial nature did adorn.
    And that all may well conclude, it could not be,
That for the place where any man was born,
    So long, and mortally, could disagree
So many nations, as for Homer striv'd,
    Unless his spur in them, had been divine.
Then end their strife, and love him (thus reviv'd)
    As born in England: see him over-shine
All other-country poets; and trust this,
    That whose-soever muse dares use her wing
When his muse flies, she will be truss'd by his;
    And show as if a barnacle should spring
Beneath an eagle . . .

The Sixth Book of Homer's Iliads

The Argument
The gods now leaving an indifferent field,
The Greeks prevail, the slaughter'd Trojans yield.
Hector (by Helenus' advice) retires
In haste to Troy and Hecuba desires
To pray Minerva to remove from fight
The son of Tydeus, her affected knight
And vow to her (for favour of such price)
Twelve oxen should be slain in sacrifice.
In mean space, Glaucus and Tydides meet
And either other with remembrance greet
Of old love 'twixt their fathers, which inclines
Their hearts to friendship, who change arms for signs
Of a continu'd love for either's life.
Hector, in his return, meets with his wife

And taking in his armed arms his son,
He prophesies the fall of Ilion.

[lines 408-567]

[Hector] went to see
The virtuous princess, his true wife, white-arm'd Andromache.
She (with her infant son and maid) was climb'd the tower, about
The sight of him that fought for her, weeping and crying out.
Hector, not finding her at home, was going forth, retir'd,
Stood in the gate, her woman call'd and curiously enquir'd
Where she was gone, bade tell him true if she were gone to see
His sisters or his brothers' wives, or whether she should be
At temple with the other dames t'implore Minerva's ruth.

   Her woman answer'd: since he ask'd and urg'd so much the truth,
The truth was she was neither gone to see his brothers' wives,
His sisters, nor t'implore the ruth of Pallas on their lives,
But she (advertis'd of the bane Troy suffer'd and how vast
Conquest had made herself for Greece), like one distraught, made haste

To ample Ilion with her son and nurse, and all the way
Mourn'd and dissolv'd in tears for him. Then Hector made no stay
But trod her path and through the streets (magnificently built)
All the great city pass'd and came where (seeing how blood was spilt)
Andromache might see him come, who made as he would pass
The ports without saluting her, not knowing where she was.
She, with his sight, made breathless haste to meet him, she, whose grace

Brought him withal so great a dower, she that of all the race
Of King Aetion only liv'd—Aetion whose house stood
Beneath the mountain Placius, environ'd with the wood
Of Theban Hypoplace, being court to the Cilician land.
She ran to Hector and with her (tender of heart and hand)
Her son borne in his nurse's arms, when like a heavenly sign
Compact of many golden stars the princely child did shine,
Whom Hector call'd Scamandrius but whom the town did name
Astyanax because his sire did only prop the same.
Hector, though grief bereft his speech, yet smil'd upon his joy.

Andromache cried out, mix'd hands and to the strength of Troy
Thus wept forth her affection: 'O noblest in desire,
Thy mind, inflam'd with others' good, will set thy self on fire,
Nor pitiest thou thy son, nor wife, who must thy widow be
If now thou issue: all the field will only run on thee.
Better my shoulders underwent the earth than thy decease,
For then would earth bear joys no more—then comes the black

                                                                                            increase

Of griefs (like Greeks on Ilion). Alas, what one survives
To be my refuge? One black day bereft seven brothers' lives
By stern Achilles; by his hand my father breath'd his last;
His high-wall'd rich Cilician Thebes sack'd by him and laid waste.
The royal body yet he left unspoil'd—religion charm'd
That act of spoil—and all in fire he burn'd him complete arm'd.
Built over him a royal tomb, and to the monument
He left of him th'Oreades (that are the high descent
Of aegis-bearing Jupiter) another of their own
Did add to it and set it round with elms: by which is shown
(In theirs) the barrenness of death; yet might it serve beside
To shelter the sad monument from all the ruffinous pride
Of storms and tempests, us'd to hurt things of that noble kind.
The short life yet my mother liv'd he sav'd, and serv'd his mind
With all the riches of the realm, which not enough esteem'd,
He kept her prisoner, whom small time but much more wealth

                                                                                                 redeem'd,

And she in sylvan Hypoplace Cilicia rul'd again,
But soon was overrul'd by death—Diana's chaste disdain
Gave her a lance and took her life. Yet all these gone from me
Thou amply render'st all: thy life makes still my father be,
My mother, brothers—and besides thou art my husband too,
Most lov'd, most worthy. Pity then, dear love, and do not go,
For, thou gone, all these go again: pity our common joy,
Lest (of a father's patronage, the bulwark of all Troy)
Thou leav'st him a poor widow's charge; stay, stay then in this tower
And call up to the wild fig-tree all thy retired power,
For there the wall is easiest seal'd and fittest for surprise:
And there th'Ajaces, Idomen, th'Atrides, Diomed thrice

Have both survey'd and made attempt—I know not if induc'd
By some wise augur, or the fact was naturally infus'd
Into their wits or courages.' To this great Hector said:
'Be well assur'd, wife, all these things in my kind cares are weigh'd:
But what a shame and fear it is to think how Troy would scorn
(Both in her husbands and her wives, whom long-train'd gowns adorn)
That I should cowardly fly off! The spirit I first did breathe
Did never teach me that—much less since the contempt of death
Was settl'd in me and my mind knew what a worthy was,
Whose office is to lead in fight and give no danger pass
Without improvement. In this fire must Hector's trial shine.
Here must his country, father, friends be in him made divine.
And such a stormy day shall come, in mind and soul I know,
When sacred Troy shall shed her towers for tears of overthrow,
When Priam, all his birth and power, shall in those tears be drown'd.
But neither Troy's posterity so much my soul doth wound—
Priam, nor Hecuba herself, nor all my brothers' woes
(Who, though so many and so good, must all be food for foes)—
As thy sad state, when some rude Greek shall lead thee weeping hence,
These free days clouded and a night of captive violence
Loading thy temples, out of which thine eyes must never see
But spin the Greek wives webs of task and their fetch-water be
To Argos, from Messeides, or clear Hyperia's spring—
Which (howsoever thou abhorr'st) fate's such a shrewish thing
She will be mistress, whose curst hands, when they shall crush out cries
From thy oppressions (being beheld by other enemies)
Thus they will nourish thy extremes: 'This dame was Hector's wife,
A man that, at the wars of Troy, did breathe the worthiest life
Of all their army.' This again will rub thy fruitful wounds
To miss the man that to thy bands could give such narrow bounds.
But that day shall not wound mine eyes: the solid heap of night
Shall interpose and stop mine ears against thy plaints and plight.'

This said, he reach'd to take his son, who (of his arms afraid,
And then the horse-hair plume, with which he was so overlaid,
Nodded so horribly) he cling'd back to his nurse and cried.
Laughter affected his great sire, who doff'd and laid aside
His fearful helm, that on the earth cast round about it light.

Then took and kiss'd his loving son and (balancing the weight
In dancing him) these loving vows to living Jove he us'd
And all the other bench of gods: 'O you that have infus'd
Soul to this infant, now set down this blessing on his star.
Let his renown be clear as mine, equal his strength in war,
And make his reign so strong in Troy that years to come may yield
His facts this fame (when, rich in spoils, he leaves the conquer'd field
Sown with his slaughters): "These high deeds exceed his father's
                                                            worth."
And let this echo'd praise supply the comforts to come forth
Of his kind mother with my life.' This said, th'heroic sire
Gave him his mother, whose fair eyes fresh streams of love's salt fire
Billow'd on her soft cheeks to hear the last of Hector's speech,
In which his vows compris'd the sum of all he did beseech
In her wish'd comfort. So she took into her odorous breast
Her husband's gift; who (mov'd to see her heart so much opprest)
He dried her tears and thus desir'd: 'Afflict me not, dear wife,
With these vain griefs. He doth not live that can disjoin my life
And this firm bosom but my fate—and fate, whose wings can fly?
Noble, ignoble, fate controls: once born, the best must die.
Go home and set thy houswifery on these extremes of thought,
And drive war from them with thy maids: keep them from doing
                                                            nought.
These will be nothing: leave the cares of war to men and me,
In whom (of all the Ilian race) they take their high'st degree.'
  On went his helm; his princess home, half cold with kindly fears,
When every fear turn'd back her looks, and every look shed tears,
Foe-slaughtering Hector's house soon reach'd; her many women there
Wept all to see her: in his life great Hector's funerals were—
Never look'd any eye of theirs to see their lord safe home,
Scap'd from the grips and powers of Greece. And now was Paris come
From his high towers, who made no stay when once he had put on
His richest armour, but flew forth; the flints he trod upon
Sparkled with lustre of his arms; his long-ebb'd spirits now flow'd
The higher for their lower ebb. And as a fair steed, proud
With full-given mangers, long tied up and now (his head-stall broke)
He breaks from stable, runs the field and with an ample stroke

Measures the centre, neighs and lifts aloft his wanton head,
About his shoulders shakes his crest, and where he hath been fed
Or in some calm flood wash'd or (stung with his high plight) he flies
Amongst his females, strength puts forth, his beauty beautifies,
And like life's mirror bears his gait—so Paris from the tower
Of lofty Pergamus came forth; he show'd a sun-like power
In carriage of his goodly parts, address'd now to the strife,
And found his noble brother near the place he left his wife.
Him (thus respected) he salutes: 'Right worthy, I have fear
That your so serious haste to field my stay hath made forbear,
And that I come not as you wish.' He answer'd: 'Honour'd man,
Be confident, for not myself nor any others can
Reprove in thee the work of fight—at least not any such
As is an equal judge of things, for thou hast strength as much
As serves to execute a mind very important. But
Thy strength too readily flies off: enough will is not put
To thy ability. My heart is in my mind's strife sad
When Troy (out of her much distress she and her friends have had
By thy procurement) doth deprave thy noblesse in mine ears.
But come, hereafter we shall calm these hard conceits of theirs
When (from their ports the foe expuls'd) high Jove to them hath given
Wish'd peace, and us free sacrifice to all the powers of heaven.'

from EUGENIA
or True Nobility's Trance, for death of the most religiously noble
William Lord Russell, &c.

Inductio

Eugenia, seeing true noblesse of no price,
Nought noble now, but servile avarice,
Loathing the baseness, high states even profess,
And loaded with an ominous heaviness:
She flew for comfort to her sister Fame;
Of whose most ancient house, the brazen frame
In midst of all the universe doth shine,

'Twixt earth, the seas, and all those tracts divine,
That are the confines of the triple world;
Through whose still open gates are ceaseless hurl'd,
The sounds of all things, breaking air in earth;
Where all men's acts are seen, each death, and birth.
Eugenia, here arriv'd; her sister gave
All entertainment she could wish to have;
Through all her palace led her, hand in hand:
Show'd her chief rooms to her, and bade command
The best of those chief, and would have her choose:
Each chief, had divers, fit for different use,
All with inscriptions of divine device
In every chamber's curious frontispiece.
Besides the names of every family,
Ennobled for effects of piety.
Virtue and valour; none that purchas'd name,
By any base course touch'd at t'house of fame;
Nor those that touch'd there, stay'd there, if they lost
The worth first in them, though they kept their boast:
Such vanish like the sea's inflated waves,
Each chase out other, and their foam's their graves.
Amongst the solid then, that there endur'd;
Eugenia (even by subtle fate allur'd)
Choos'd an inscription, that did highly please
Seeing in fine gold graven, the Russelides:
Fame prais'd her choice, and said, the name was given
By sacred purpose and presage of heaven,
Expressing in the birth, th'antiquity
Of that most virtue season'd family,
The word importing an effect of age,
And long-liv'd labour; proving the presage,
That foresaw actions, which should labours be,
Wrinkl'd with time, and aged industry.
She here repos'd, and from the base world gone,
To cheer her earthly desolation,
The heralds, and the registers of fame,
Of life and death, and all things worth the name,

(Th'ingenuous muses) follow'd, and with them
The cheerful graces: and of each extreme,
The parting virtues: of all which, not one
Would stay, when she, that grac'd them all was gone.
Religion flew before, for she being ground
And root to all acts, noble and renown'd,
Their veins bleed never, but hers, first have vent,
She's their plain form, and they her ornament.
All these together now in fame's old house,
Which (though of brass) is yet most ruinous,
They saw the sun look pale, and cast through air,
Discolour'd beams; nor could he paint so fair,
Heaven's bow in dewy vapours, but he left
The greater part unform'd; the circle cleft,
And like a bull's neck short'ned; no hues seen,
But only one, and that was wat'rish green:
His heat was chok'd up, as in ovens compress'd
Half stifling men; heaven's drooping face was dress'd
In gloomy thunderstrokes: earth, seas, array'd
In all presage of storm: the bitterns play'd
And met in flocks; the herons set clamours gone,
That rattled up air's triple region.
The cormorants to dry land did address,
And cried away, all fowls that us'd the seas.
The wanton swallows jerk'd the standing springs
Met in dull lakes; and flew so close, their wings
Shav'd the top waters: frogs croak'd; the swart crow
Measur'd the sea-sands, with pace passing slow,
And often sous'd her ominous heat of blood
Quite over head and shoulders in the flood,
Still scolding at the rain's so slow access:
The trumpet-throated, the Naupliades,
Their clangers threw about, and summon'd up
All clouds to crown imperious tempest's cup:
The erring dolphin puff'd the foamy main
Hither and thither, and did upwards rain:
The raven sat belching out his funeral din,

Venting his voice, with sucking of it in.
The patient of all labours, the poor ant
Her eggs to caves brought: molehills proof did want
To keep such tears out, as heav'n now would weep.
The hundred-footed canker-worms did creep
Thick on the wet walls. The slow crab did take
Pebbles into her mouth, and ballast make
Of gravel, for her stay, against the gales,
Close clinging to the shore. Sea-giant whales
The watery mountains darted at the sky.
And (no less ominous) the petulant fly
Bit bitterly for blood, as then most sweet.
The loving dog digg'd earth up with his feet,
The ass (as weather wise) confirm'd these fears,
And never left shaking his flaggy ears.
Th'ingenious bee wrought ever near her hive.
The cloddy ashes, kept coals long alive,
And dead coals quicken'd; both transparent clear:
The rivers crown'd with swimming feathers were.
The trees' green fleeces flew about the air
And aged thistles lost their downy hair,
Cattle would run from out their shed undriven,
To th'ample pastures: lambs were sprightly given,
And all in jumps about the short leas borne:
Rams fiercely butted, locking horn in horn.
The storm now near: those cattle that abroad
Undriven ran from their shelter; undriven, trod
Homewards as fast: the large bon'd oxen look'd
Oft on the broad heaven, and the soft air suck'd,
Smelling it in; their reeking nostrils still
Sucking the clear dew from the daffodil:
Bow'd to their sides their broad heads, and their hair
Lick'd smooth at all parts; lov'd their night-tide lair:
And late in night, did bellow from the stall,
As thence the tempest would his blasts exhale.
The swine, her never made bed now did ply
And with her snout strew'd every way her sty,

The wolf howl'd in her den; th'insatiate beast,
Now fearing no man, met him breast to breast,
And like a murd'rous beggar, him allur'd;
Haunting the home-groves husbandmen manur'd.
Then night her circle clos'd; and shut in day,
Her silver spangles shedding every way
And earth's poor stars (the glow-worms) lay abroad
As thick as heaven's; that now no twinkle show'd,
Sudden'stly plucking in their guilty heads.
And forth the winds brake, from their brazen beds
That struck the mountains so, they cried quite out.
The thunder chid; the lightning leapt about;
And clouds so gush'd, as Iris ne'er were shown
But in fresh deluge, heav'n itself came down:
Yet all this was not, half due ominous state
To lead so great and consequent a fate,
As took from us, this rare religious lord . . .

EPILOGUE TO THE HYMNS OF HOMER

The work that I was born to do, is done.
Glory to him, that the conclusion
Makes the beginning of my life: and never
Let me be said to live; till I live ever.

   Where's the outliving of my fortunes then,
Ye errant vapours of fame's Lernean fen?
That (like possess'd storms) blast all; not in herd
With your abhorr'd heads: who, because cashier'd
By men, for monsters; think men, monsters all,
That are not of your pied hood, and your hall.
When you are nothing but the scum of things,
And must be cast off: drones, that have no stings,
Nor any more soul, than a stone hath wings.

   Avaunt ye hags; your hates, and scandals are,
The crowns, and comforts of a good man's care;
By whose impartial perpendicular

All is extuberance, and tumor all,
That you your ornaments, and glories call.
Your wry mouths censure right? your blister'd tongues,
That lick but itches? and whose ulcerous lungs
Come up at all things permanent, and sound?
O you (like flies in dregs) in humours drown'd;
Your loves, like atoms, lost in gloomy air;
I would not retrieve with a wither'd hair.
Hate, and cast still your stings then; for your kisses
Betray but truth; and your applauds, are hisses.

   To see our supercilious wizards frown;
Their faces fall'n like frogs; and coming down,
Stinking the sun out; make me shine the more:
And like a check'd flood, bear above the shore,
That their profane opinions fain would set,
To what they see not; know not; nor can let.
Yet then, our learn'd men, with their torrents come
Roaring from their forc'd hills, all crown'd with foam,
That one not taught like them, should learn to know
Their Greek roots, and from thence the groves that grow,
Casting such rich shades, from great Homer's wings:
That first, and last, command the muses' springs.
Though he's best scholar, that through pains and vows;
Made his own master only; all things knows.
Nor pleads my poor skill; form; or learned place;
But dauntless labour, constant prayer, and grace.
And what's all their skill, but vast varied reading?
As if broad-beaten highways had the leading
To truth's abstract, and narrow path, and pit?
Found in no walk, of any worldly wit.
And without truth; all's only sleight of hand,
Or our law-learning, in a foreign land;
Embroidery spent on cobwebs; braggart show
Of men that all things learn; and nothing know.
For ostentation, humble truth still flies,
And all confederate fashionists, defies.
And as some sharp-brow'd doctor, (English-born;)

In much learn'd Latin idioms can adorn
A verse with rare attractions; yet become
His English muse, like an Arachnean loom,
Wrought spite of Pallas; and therein bewrays
More tongue than truth; begs, and adopts his bays;
So ostentation, be he never so
Larded with labour, to suborn his show;
Shall sooth within him, but a bastard soul,
No more heaven heiring, than earth's son, the mole.
But as in dead calms, emptiest smokes arise
Uncheck'd and free; up, straight into the skies;
So drowsy peace, that in her humour steeps
All she affects, lets such rise while she sleeps.
Many, and most men, have of wealth least store,
But none the gracious shame that fits the poor;
So most learn'd men, enough are ignorant;
But few the grace have, to confess their want,
Till lives, and learnings, come concomitant.
For from men's knowledges; their lives' acts flow;
Vainglorious acts then, vain prove all they know.
As night, the life-inclining stars, best shows;
So lives obscure, the starriest souls disclose.

   For me; let just men judge by what I show
In acts expos'd, how much I err, or know;
And let not envy, make all worse than nought
With her mere headstrong, and quite brainless thought:
Others, for doing nothing; giving all;
And bounding all worth in her bursten gall.

   God and my dear Redeemer, rescue me
From men's immane, and mad impiety;
And by my life and soul, (sole known to them)
Make me of palm, or yew, an anadem.
And so, my sole God, the thrice sacred Trine,
Bear all th'ascription, of all me and mine.

Supplico tibi Domine, Pater et Dux rationis nostrae; ut nostrae nobilitatis recordemur, qua tu nos ornasti; et ut tu nobis presto sis, ut eis qui per sese moventur; ut et a corporis contagio, Brutorumque affectuum repurgemur; eosque superemus, atque regamus; et, sicut decet; pro instrumentis eis utamur. Deinde, ut nobis adiumento sis; ad accuratam rationis nostrae correctionem; et conjunctionem cum eis qui vere sunt, per lucem veritatis. Et tertium, Salvatori supplex oro; ut ab oculis animorum nostrorum, caliginem prorsus abstergas; ut norimus bene, qui Deus, aut mortalis habendus, *Amen.*